THE UNIVERSITY OF WEST FLORIDA

3 2100 00336 5178

AF323959

MICROCOMPUTERS IN DEVELOPMENT:
A Manager's Guide

Noel Berge, Marcus D. Ingle, and Marcia Hamilton

Kumarian Press

DEDICATION

To all the unsung professionals in developing country ministries,
enterprises, and donor organizations who are overloaded with data and
inefficient means of information processing.

Copyright © 1986 by Kumarian Press
630 Oakwood Avenue, Suite 119, West Hartford, Connecticut 06110

All rights reserved. No part of this publication may be reproduced,
stored in a retrieval system, or transmitted in any form, or by any
means, electronic, mechanical, photocopying, recording, or otherwise,
without prior written permission by the publisher.

Printed in the United States of America

Cover design by Marilyn Penrod

This first edition of Microcomputers in Management was prepared on a
Kaypro computer in WordStar. For the revised edition, those files were
converted to MS DOS to be used with Word Perfect and printed on a
Printers Plus laser printer in Epson elite type.

Library of Congress Cataloging in Publication Data

Berge, Noel, 1943–
   Microcomputers in Development

Rev. ed. of Microcomputers in Development/
 Marcus D. Ingle, Noel Berge, Marcia Hamilton

    Bibliography: p:
    1.Microcomputers. 2.Economic development projects––
Management––Data Processing. I. Ingle, Marcus. II. Hamilton, Marcia,
1943–   III. Ingle, Marcus. Microcomputers in Development. IV.
Title.

QA76.5.B423 1986   658.4'038   86-10539
ISBN 0-931816-05-X

TABLE OF CONTENTS

iii

THE LIBRARY
UNIVERSITY OF WEST FLORIDA

Appendices

Figures

Tables

AUTHORS' PREFACE (2ND EDITION)

We are still in the midst of a microcomputer revolution. But many things have changed since the writing of the first edition of the Guide. In development and development management, the use of the microcomputer is causing a revolution in organizational control, information sharing, participatory management and decentralization.

The Guide's original audience included first-time users and related professionals who were beginning to recognize the microcomputer's use in enhancing efficiency and productivity in their work. This group was on the forefront of buying and introducing microcomputers in development and Third World situations. That group is no longer small, and has become sufficiently diffused throughout organizations and project management that the microcomputer is seen as a powerful tool that is of great value in the management process.

Therefore, in the second edition, we have addressed still another audience: experienced microcomputer users who are interested in upgrading their systems, networking them and ensuring that they are sustainable and productive over the long run. Today's microcomputers are literally hundreds of times more powerful, faster, easier to use in a variety of situations, and affordable. Even as we write this preface, the new generation of software has become "intelligent," the hardware and operating systems are changing, and the technology moves faster than ever. In addition, the user--the professional and the manager--has increasingly become aware of how and where the microcomputer can contribute to an organization's success.

The focus has shifted: whereas in the past we primarily addressed the individual user, now we look at the use of the microcomputer from an organizational perspective. This change will radically affect many organizations, bringing increases in productivity and releases in creativity when addressing the pressing issues in development.

We hope that development managers--including host-country professionals, donor agency personnel, and international contractors and consultants--all view this revised edition of the Guide as one of several information sources to be consulted when choosing and using microcomputers in development management.

Noel Berge
Marcus Ingle
Marcia Hamilton

ACKNOWLEDGEMENTS

The first edition of the Manager's Guide was based on research sponsored by the Development Project Management Center (DPMC), Technical Assistance Division, Office of International Cooperation and Development, USDA under the Performance Management Project (#936-5317). In April 1983 "Acquiring and Using Microcomputers in Agricultural Development: A Manager's Guide" was published by DPMC in cooperation with The International Development Management Center (IDMC), Office of International Programs, University of Maryland, College Park, MD.

During the writing of the first edition, we received input and support from many individuals and institutions working in international development. Morris Solomon of DPMC reviewed the text and offered excellent suggestions for both focus and clarification. Additional DPMC assistance came from Dr. Merlyn Kettering, Pierette Countryman, Patti Lowery, and Pat Isman. Thanks, also, to Dr. Kenneth Kornher, Jeanne North, Duncan Miller, Dr. Edwin Connerly, Dr. Carl Gotsch, Ronald Steele, Edward Rizzo, Junko Olson, Gwen Salters, Eloise Altes, and Jim Davis.

So much has changed in microcomputer technology since the Guide's first edition was published. Although it had gone through three printings, and had become somewhat dated, we hesitated for over a year on the decision to produce a revised edition. Meanwhile, development professionals continued to request copies. These requests, plus some gentle prodding from our publisher, prevailed. I initiated the production process, and took the lead in the writing. Marcus offered many excellent suggestions and made substantial revisions on the initial and last chapters. Marcia's experience in Thailand added substance to our updated section on training and the computer management process. Marcia also deserves recognition for keeping a copy of the book on disk and expediting the revision process by sending it to Thunder from Thailand.

With three authors out of the country on an irregular basis, the staff at Thunder and Associates must be commended for coordinating and organizing the production effort. Lizabeth Shay played the key role in the writing and editing process: she literally re-edited the first edition and provided the necessary expertise to update the Guide's technical information. More so, Liz's involvement brought continuity to the work, and deserves recognition beyond her role of technical support/revision. Judy Light contributed much of the final editing and general support. Ken Ribyat offered technical advice based on his field experience. Finally, Monica Reyes deserves mention for providing administrative back-stop and logistical support.

Thanks to the authors of the case studies for developing their cases in the format required. Thanks, also, to Jerry Glenn of Partnership for Productivity for updating our information on Carinet.

Thanks to Krishna Sondhi, our publisher, for making it happen, again; to Meera Handa, for keeping Thunder's Kenya office going, and allowing time to write instead of dealing with brush fires; to Marcia Hamilton's support group in Thailand; to IDMC, especially Ken Smith and Artie Kennedy; to the staff at Printers Plus; and to my wife, Nancy, for being there, both personally and professionally.

Noel Berge
Alexandria, Virginia

INTRODUCTION

In Kenya recently, several donor agency personnel, Ministry officials, and one of the authors were discussing development. Inevitably, they talked about microcomputers. One member of the group mentioned that he was ordering an IBM PC to help him write reports. A high-ranking government official commented that foreigners seemed to be crazed by jogging and "microprocessors"--the local term for microcomputers. The official asked why so many people were purchasing microcomputers. Was this only another Western fad or was this the beginning of a new microelectronic era?

Indeed, microcomputer advocates may have difficulty understanding why many people do not share their zeal for electronic equipment. Providing officials with evidence of the utility of microcomputers can be a delicate and difficult task, particularly if there is some fear that people will be put out of work. Conversely, persuading overly enthusiastic officials of the problems that arise when installing computer systems may be an equally arduous undertaking. Donor, contractor, and host-country personnel must be involved in the entire decision-making process if microcomputers are to be accepted and appropriately used within project or institutional settings.

Today a $4,000 desk-top computer system can perform functions that would have cost one million dollars to execute in 1950. This tremendous reduction in cost has been accompanied by other profound changes, many of which have occurred within the last few years. The microcomputer represents a significant advance in computer technology, both in terms of reductions in the cost of computer power and the ease with which the system itself can be used. Important technological advances include:

- o the development of inexpensive, high-powered memory devices in very small "chips" that are much sturdier than previous devices;

- o the increased reliability and durability of microcomputers, attributable to the reliability of components and modular construction;

- o the proliferation of relatively low-cost software programs that enable non-programmers, including managers, to make effective use of computers with relatively little training;

- o the potential to network single-user systems with other microcomputers, minicomputers and mainframes for more computing power and storage capacity.

SOME IMPLICATIONS

The implications for managers are far-reaching. For large and complex projects, it is clear that the mere mechanics of entering and computing data manually is a formidable obstacle to better management, particularly in countries with meager pools of skilled workers. The advantage of using a microcomputer in such circumstances has been so obvious, and so desirable, to a number of managers working in developing countries, that they purchased microcomputers with their own funds and used them to achieve more effective results. Research that supports the findings and recommendations reported here relies heavily on the experience of these early microcomputer users.

But as we shift from limited to wide-spread use of microcomputers, we must consider the effects of such proliferation on human resources and look closely at the question of potential labor displacement. If, indeed, a microcomputer is like a cadre of efficient and accurate workers working overtime to get the job done, what happens to the people who could be employed in its stead? The proliferation of the new technology will present many dilemmas to which there are no simple answers. Circumstances will dictate how the issues will be resolved.

There is one circumstance in which the case for using microcomputers is obvious: this is where skilled personnel are scarce and the microcomputer becomes the primary option for processing the information necessary to achieve development objectives. In the Sahel, for example, using a microcomputer to do the work of a number of people is a clear-cut solution to personnel shortages. The choice is less obvious in developing countries with substantial pools of educated and skilled persons available to work as support staff.

The issue of employment remains a primary consideration in whether you should acquire a microcomputer for your management purposes. Indeed, purchasing a microcomputer, retraining existing staff, or hiring additional staff are three options among many for accomplishing management tasks.

WHAT A MICROCOMPUTER IS NOT

Nevertheless, the microcomputer can be highly efficient and, given its capabilities, it is not difficult to understand why it is becoming as indispensible as the pencil, the pocket calculator, and the telephone. Many stateside managers cannot work without their computers. However, placing a microcomputer in a Third World setting may present many problems. Throughout this Guide we will attempt to establish a careful balance between the advantages and disadvantages of using a microcomputer in a development project setting. It is important to look at computer capability in a realistic manner, to consider what the microcomputer <u>cannot</u> do for you, and to assess and understand the limits of the technology as they apply to development and your job.

When considering the use of microcomputers in development, it is
important to realize that the microcomputer:

o   will not make you more organized;

o   will not make decisions for you;

o   will not improve your basic data (i.e. junk in, junk
     out);

o   does not accept responsibility for anything;

o   does not do forecasting and trend analysis (but
     helps you do it);

o   cannot define problems or set objectives.

<u>You</u> are still the most important part of the system. No matter how
fast your computer can come up with the information you need, you still
have to decide what to do with that information. It takes time and
money to set up a system. It takes time to become trained even in the
most easy-to-use software programs. The microcomputer can help you and
your staff perform routine tasks. It can help you plan and account for
expenditures, but whether a system will really work for you depends on
the information you put into it, the computer's integration into the
work setting, and an environment conducive to its functioning properly.
Only you can assess whether or not these conditions can be met.

WHO SHOULD USE THIS GUIDE?

This Guide is intended for development personnel who are associated
with the management of projects or institutions. It is written for
individual managers, management teams, and related support personnel
who are likely to purchase a single-user microcomputer or who already
have one and are interested in expanding and sustaining its use in a
development organization. The Guide will provide host-country, donor
agency, and contract managers with relevant information about
microcomputer acquisition, installation, and use.

To determine if the Guide will be useful to you, ask yourself the
following questions:

o   Are you a development professional who resides in or
     frequently travels to developing countries?

o   Are you a member of a developing country, donor or
     contractor organization with some management or
     administrative responsibility?

3

o   Are you considering purchasing or upgrading and
    integrating a stand-alone microcomputer system and
    using it in development work?

o   Are you long a believer in, or recently intrigued by,
    the potential of microcomputers for improving
    organizational efficiency and quality of work?

If you answered "yes" to at least three of these questions, including
the final one, then there is a high probability that you will find this
Guide to be both of interest and value. In Figure 1 below you would
fit into the shaded area of the diagram--the area represented by the
Guide's intended audience. However, if you only answered one of the
questions positively, you may find some segment of the Guide valuable.

Figure 1   Graphic Representation of the Audience for the Guide

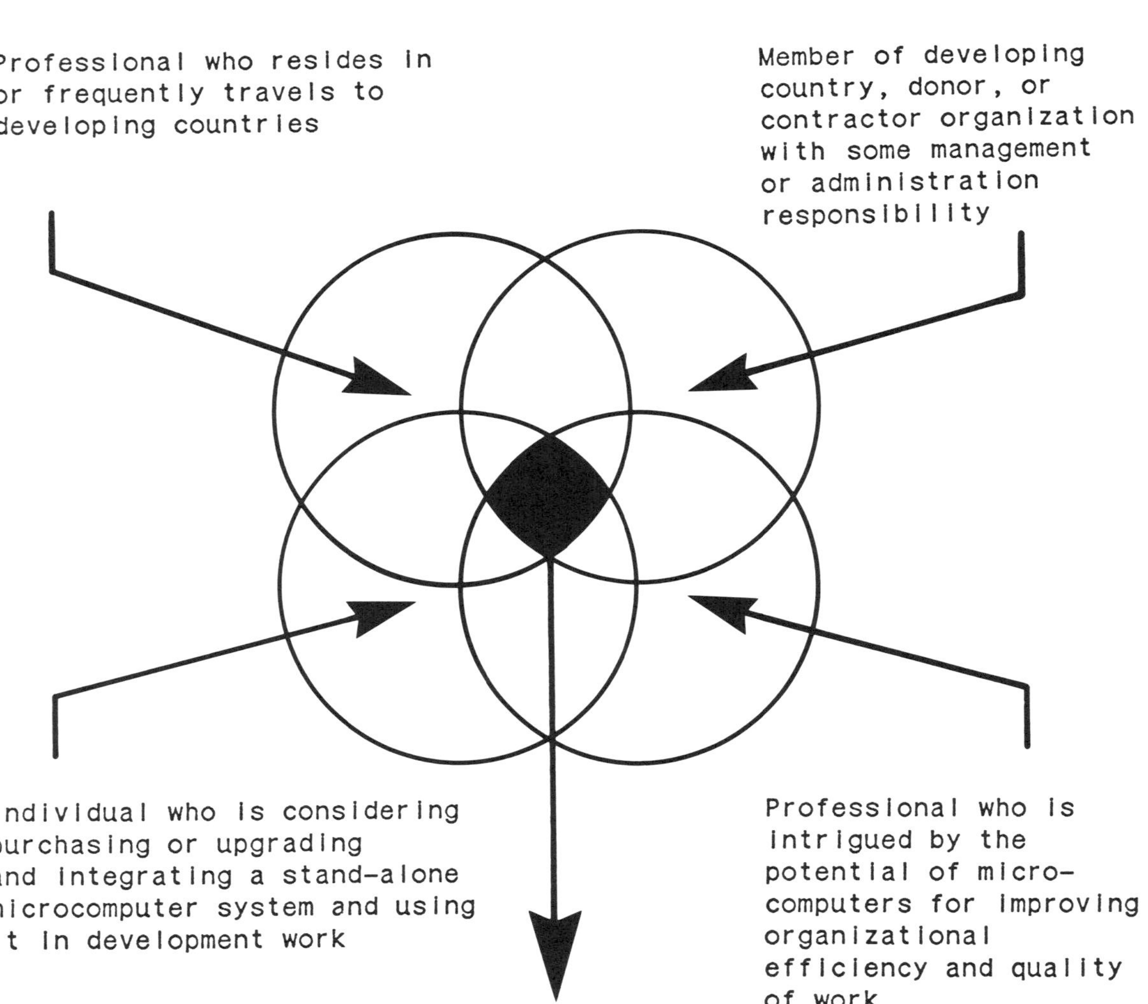

THE PURPOSE AND SCOPE OF THE GUIDE

The subject of this Guide is the appropriate selection and intelligent use of microcomputers in the management of development projects and institutions in developing countries. The operational question is not whether microcomputers will be introduced in development settings, but rather, when and how they can be suitably introduced and productively used to improve the performance of development projects and institutions.

Terminology

Normally, programs and projects are distinguished from each other with a program defined as an aggregate of projects. In this Guide, however, we refer to programs as synonymous with projects, mainly to eliminate confusion between the nomenclature of development and of computer software "programs."

The Focus

The Guide focuses on single or stand-alone microcomputer systems as separate entities or as components of larger networked systems; it does not focus on larger systems and their operations as such. Thus, it should be read as an introductory sourcebook for potential and actual microcomputer users who want to know the answers to several basic questions.

o   What can a microcomputer do?

o   What management needs can be met by a microcomputer system?

o   What software is available for different management requirements?

o   What environmental problems affect system hardware?

o   What system hardware is available?

o   How reliable is the microcomputer?

o   What can be done in the event of a system breakdown?

o   What training is needed to operate and maintain the computer?

o   How can a microcomputer be linked to other computer systems?

Appendices are included to supplement the Guide's discussion. A glossary is provided to clarify the "jungle of jargon" used in the microcomputer field. Lists of information sources and materials on microcomputers that are relevant to circumstances in developing countries are also provided.

WHAT THE GUIDE DOES AND DOES NOT DO

With guides of this type, the reader's expectations may exceed the writers' intent; thus, it is useful to specify what this Guide is _not_. It is not:

o   a promotion piece for a particular kind or brand of microcomputer equipment;

o   an advocacy document for microcomputers in general, or their specific application to development management;

o   a descriptive account of the most recent technological improvements in microcomputer software and hardware;

o   an advanced manual for microcomputer specialists and technicians;

o   a comprehensive set of introductory materials for personnel interested in microcomputers but not related to development;

o   a source of information on microcomputer networking and interfacing with mini and mainframe computers.

The Guide does provide relevant information on the functions of microcomputers in development management settings, the kinds of systems that are currently in use, and a simple method for you to use in assessing your own need for a microcomputer. The Guide includes:

o   an overview of computing equipment and applications; (Chapter I)

o   potential applications of microcomputers in the management of development projects and institutions; (Chapter I)

o   the concept and importance of microcomputer user-friendliness; (Chapter II)

o   a description of microcomputer software programs and hardware components; (Chapter II)

o suggestions for assessing your need for a microcomputer
   in terms of work, environment, and personal
   requirements, including pros and cons of microcomputers
   in developing country situations; (Chapter III)

o a discussion of the acquisition, installation, and use
   of microcomputer systems; (Chapter IV)

o case histories and applications of microcomputers used
   in managing development projects; (Chapter V)

o the strengths and limitations of microcomputers;
   (Chapter VI)

o future trends of microcomputers in development;
   (Chapter VI)

o computer glossary, lists of publications and
   manufacturers of hardware and software. (Appendices)

Microcomputers offer an unprecedented opportunity for humans to
increase their involvement and participation in the creative aspects of
management; the machines can take over a large part of the drudgery of
sorting information and statistical analysis. The microcomputer
represents a giant step toward the greater use of human capacities. If
used appropriately in developing countries, it can be of immense help
in ensuring efficient use of scarce resources. The purpose of this
Guide is to explore, define, describe, and help you assess the meaning
of "appropriate" in your situation.

CHAPTER I
Microcomputer Systems
and Development Management

The microcomputer is a workhorse in a desk-top design. With the right combination of hardware and software it is easy to use, easy to understand, and forgiving. This ease of use (known as user-friendliness) is due to the unique attributes of microcomputer hardware and to software that is intentionally designed for non-technical persons. Every individual--not just the specialized operator--can use a microcomputer to do various work-related tasks from number crunching, to report writing, to data filing and storing. As a result, the microcomputer is generating a revolution in the thinking and practice of human, physical, and information resource management in many international development settings.

OVERVIEW OF COMPUTING EQUIPMENT AND APPLICATIONS

The computer family includes super computers, mainframes, minis, micros, and several others with esoteric names. Our focus is on the small single-user computer--the microcomputer--that includes the keyboard, the central processing unit, the memory, the monitor, the disk drives and the printer. Portable models are available that are the size of an attache case or smaller. Thus, although several different people may use it at different times, the microcomputer is a small computer used by one person at a time to perform specific tasks.

Before considering the implications of the user-friendliness of micro-computer systems, it is helpful to consider microcomputers in the context of computing systems generally. In Figure 2, (Range of Computing Capability and Potential Applications for Computer Equip-ment) we display types of computers and types of users and refer to microcomputers as "personal single-user," "professional single-user," and "professional multi-user." We have organized computers into five categories from low to high range of computing capability and have noted a few systems under each category. They are displayed by single versus multi-user and system capability.

In Figure 2, we group various "computing" machines according to their ability to do a number of different kinds of tasks. We make the assumption that the number of applications and memory size are the two most important features of capability. For example, the hand-held calculator is capable of doing many sophisticated calculations, it is used by only one person at a time, and has no (or a very small) memory. If you need to do a few basic calculations, then a hand-held calculator is probably what you need--not a computer.

As you move from left to right on the chart, you move from less to more
computing capability. Equipment on the right subsumes the functions of
equipment on the left. Thus, you can see from Figure 2 that a typical
microcomputer can do what a calculator can do, but has more memory, and
can handle one or more users. On the right side of the spectrum are
the multi-use, multi-user computers. These are equal to or slightly
larger in memory capability than the microcomputer (in the mid range),
and more than one person can use the system at the same time. Consider
the table below in terms of the capability of the stand-alone,
multi-use, but single-user system.

Figure 2 — Range of Computing Capability and Potential Applications for Computer Equipment

RANGE OF COMPUTING CAPABILITY	Low ◄———— Mid Range ————► High				
TYPES OF COMPUTER EQUIPMENT	Programmable Calculators	Game and Home Computers	Personal/ Laptop Micro- computers	Business/ Multi-user Micro- computers	Mini and Mainframe Computers
EXAMPLE	TI 59 HP43CV	Atari 520ST Timex Sinclair, Commodore 64 IBM PC JR Kaypro II	IBM PC IBM PC XT Amiga McIntosh KaproIV/10 Tandy 600	IBM PC AT Compaq DeskPro286 TI Business Pro HP Vector	Wang VS, IBM 3370, PDP 11
RANGE OF POTENTIAL APPLICATIONS	Personal single user with limited applications ◄————►				
	Professional single-user with multiple applications ◄————————————————►				
				Professional multi-user with multiple applications ◄————►	

MICROCOMPUTERS AND DEVELOPMENT MANAGEMENT

Ideally, International development is a cooperative, evolving process
whereby countries and their peoples are better meeting their present
needs while building their capacity to meet future needs.
Notwithstanding this goal, however, development activities, including
projects and institutional development efforts, are typically situated
in harsh environments and rely for their success on the integrated
action of many different stakeholders and organizations.   The
achievement of intended (and often ambitious) objectives in the face of
frequently severe resource and time constraints requires careful
planning, implementation, and evaluation; that is, good development
management.   Management involves the economical use of human and
material resources to accomplish valued results under conditions of
uncertainty and partial control.   It involves a continuous cycle of
planning and replanning: a continuous stream of information must be
gathered, processed, reported, and acted upon.

The successful management of development efforts is highly complex, and
illustrations of serious development management deficiencies abound.
During design and analysis, incentives are typically weighted toward
getting development funding rather than toward economic and technical
feasibility.   The implementation requirements are often underestimated
or totally neglected.   As a result, the responsible managerial and
technical staff are frequently hard-pressed to do what is minimally
necessary to keep their efforts on schedule and within budget.   There
is little opportunity to move beyond routine administrative demands and
the sporadic handling of crises to creatively guide a development
effort toward its long-term objectives.   The obvious need for a more
adaptive and humanistic approach is often overwhelmed by externally
imposed deadlines, unexpected events, and most dispiriting, by tedious
and time-consuming routine administrative tasks.

While the physical, policy, and institutional factors of developing
countries are often out of the control of development managers, there
are promising technologies available for both preventing and resolving
many development management deficiencies.   These technologies, which
distinguish among and specify appropriate approaches for project
management, program management, organizational improvement, and
institutional development are now being codified and disseminated by a
number of private and public sector entities, including AID's Science
and Technology Bureau, the World Bank, the UNDP, the USDA, the
University of Maryland's International Development Management Center,
and others.

The microcomputer offers substantial promise with respect to development management potential.   Many practitioners are now turning to the
microcomputer as a tool that can play a significant role in improving
and sustaining effective development management (Ingle, et al.: 1983;
Pinckney, et al.: 1984; Woord: 1984: Zemke: 1984).   In the remainder of

this chapter we introduce a framework for examining the general and specific management potential of microcomputer systems in development situations.

<u>Generic Management Functions</u>

After reviewing the international development management literature, we found that several generic functions--manifested in terms of specific managerial tasks--are directly associated with many successful development efforts (Management Development Working Group: 1981; Ingle: 1981; Vail: 1982; DPMC, IICA and IDMC: 1983). The presence of these functions greatly increases the probability that development efforts will be successful in achieving objectives, will be completed on time, and will be within budget limits. These functions are discussed below.

1. Developing a consensus and commitment to objectives and strategies on the part of key personnel: includes developing overall policy objectives and development strategies; identifying objectives for development programs and sectoral institutions based on policies, opportunities, and targeted beneficiaries; establishing measurable performance indicators and targets for specific projects based on detailed assessments of potential benefits, feasibility, and implementation costs; and employing appropriate processes for assuring that key actors clearly understand and are committed to the objectives and strategies that have been developed.

Microcomputers can be used to provide assistance in the collection and analysis of sectoral, census and survey data; feasibility studies and analyses of project costs and benefits; and storage and presentation of information in the form of matrices, summaries, and narrative reports. The microcomputer's ability to make easy updates and revisions allows feedback to be reentered until key actors arrive at consensus on the final output.

2. Devising and agreeing upon realistic workplans, schedules, re-sources, and budgets: involves developing descriptions of activities, including input and output specifications and information on critical external conditions; developing work breakdown tables and determining realistic personnel and resource requirements; creating a master schedule and special sub-schedules for important activities; and employing a process for assuring that key managerial and technical persons understand and agree on the detailed plans.

A microcomputer's analytic capabilities are particularly useful, in that formats and specifications for performance targets, project input, output, and key external conditions can be stored and data processed in accordance with the formatted specifications. A microcomputer can also assist in the development of work breakdown diagrams and rapidly process and analyze timing and duration of activities through the preparation of critical path, network, and bar chart schedules. Microcomputer technology provides a fast, reliable, and convenient means whereby managers and technicians can jointly obtain consensus on

activities and quickly review planning data to suggest modifications
for improvement.

**3.   Defining clear roles and responsibilities for task execution and
replanning:** includes the development of plans for the assignment and
use of personnel, commodities, equipment, and supplies; the
identification of the individual or unit responsible for each activity
in the effort, ensuring understanding, incentive, and skill availability; and negotiation of the roles and responsibilities of the
various personnel involved in the effort.

Microcomputers can facilitate this process by storing, processing, and
analyzing data on various institutions and stakeholders involved in,
and affected by, the development activity as well as procedural data
pertaining to personnel, contracting, procurement, and training. The
workload of various sectors can be tracked, the balance of resource
allocation between operational units reviewed, and reports prepared for
the review of decision makers.

**4.   Appropriately directing and controlling task execution in accor-
dance with plans:** involves controlling actual work activities
according to the negotiated plans through the development and issuing
of policies, procedures, and project status, and allows for fast and
reliable modeling of contingencies based upon changes in plans or
resource availability.

**5.   Assessing progress and responding to changes in the internal and
external environment:** includes identifying information needs, sources
of data, and the means for collecting them; monitoring the development
effort's progress; exploring the implications of alternative strategies
and methods; and implementing an appropriate process whereby the
relevant actors and stakeholders receive and comprehend high-quality
feedback. Microcomputers can facilitate these actions, again by
serving as the repository of program and financial information, and as
the means to manipulate information according to various models and
usable formats.

These generic functions are related to the specific tasks and potential
microcomputer uses and products. Table 1 provides the basis for
relating the performance of specific development management tasks to
various microcomputer applications and software programs.

Table 1

Generic Management Functions Associated with Successful Management of Development Projects and Institutions	Management Tasks Related to the Generic Management Functions
I. A consensus and commitment to development objectives and strategies by key actors and stakeholders.	A. Develop overall policy objectives and development strategies through socio/political/economic/financial/technical/institutional analyses and sectoral studies. B. Identify objectives for development projects and institutions based on opportunities, and the identification of major beneficiary groups. C. Establish measurable perform-ance indicators and targets for development efforts based on detailed assessments of potential benefits, imple-mentation feasibility, and costs. D. Employ an appropriate process for assuring that key develop-ment actors clearly understand and are committed to objectives and strategies.

Typical Microcomputer Uses For Key Management Tasks	Microcomputer Products Corresponding to Various Uses
A1. Format, store, and analyze policy statements and statements of development strategies	A1a. Narrative policy descriptions A1b. Narrative and graphical strategy descriptions.
A2. Store, process and analyze agricultural, household census, and survey data.	A2a. Descriptive statistics of physical, economic, social and political conditions.
A3. Quickly analyze "what if" scenarios of various strategic options for policy implementation.	A3a. Comparative analytical tables of costs and benefits
B1. Store, process, and analyze sector and project specific problems, opportunities, and objectives	B1a. Narrative descriptions B1b. Problem diagrams B1c. Oval and tree diagrams of objectives
B2. Preliminary analysis of intended target groups "receiving" and "losing" benefits from the development activity.	B2a. Descriptive statistics of project target groups. B2b. Stakeholder matrix of major project and institutional beneficiaries.
C1. Store formats and specifications for targeting indicators in terms of intended performance and time	C1a. Project design matrix C1b. Narrative lists of benefits for each target group over time.
C2. Initial estimates of socio-economic benefits, feasibility, and costs associated with development activity.	C2a. Narrative list of key benefits and costs. C2b. Initial cost-effectiveness ratios for various project alternatives
D1. In meetings with key policy makers and project designers, microcomputer used to take process notes and provide immediate feedback on areas of consensus and divergence.	D1a. Narrative descriptive text and notes of meetings and planning sessions.

Generic Management Functions Associated with Successful Management of Development Projects and Institutions	Management Tasks Related to the Generic Management Functions
II. Realistic and agreed upon work-plans, schedules, and resource estimates.	A. Develop detailed descriptions of development activities including input and output specifications and critical external conditions. B. Break planned work into discrete units and create realistic personnel and resources requirements for each segment. C. Create a master program schedule and special subschedules for important activity sets. D. Employ an appropriate process for assuring that key managerial and technical persons understand and agree on the detailed execution arrangements.

Typical Microcomputer Uses for Key Management Tasks	Microcomputer Products Corresponding to Various Uses
A1. Store formats and specifications for developing performance targets for development program inputs, and key external conditions.	A1a. Input/output activity templates
A2. Store, process, and organize input/output data in accordance with formatted specifications.	A2a. Completed input/output activity templates.
B1. Store and process task/work performance data associated with development efforts.	B1a. Narrative listing of key activities along with dependent prior and subsequent events.
B2. Allocate personnel and material resources by output category, work task, and sub-activities.	B2a. Resource allocation charts and diagrams.
C1. Process and analyze timing and duration of project and organizational activities.	C1a. Critical path and network schedules. C1b. Bar chart schedules.
D1. Provide a fast, low-cost and convenient means whereby managers and technicians can list activity, cost, and time data and negotiate realistic agreements.	D1a. Activity workplans jointly developed by and agreed to by key planners and implementors.
D2. Provide quick and efficient means whereby supervisors and colleagues can quickly review planning data and suggest modifications/improvements	D2a. Revised workplans.

Generic Management Functions Associated with Successful Management of Development Projects and Institutions	Management Tasks Related to the Generic Management Functions
III. Clearly articulated and understood structures, roles and responsibilities for executing development activities and tasks.	A. Develop plans for the assignment and use of personnel, commodities, equipment, and supplies. B. For each activity and subactivity identify responsible units and individuals and assure there is a clear understanding of work and technical skills required to perform the task. C. Negotiate roles and responsibilities with various personnel involved in development efforts at multiple echelons and in related operational units. D. Employ an appropriate process for assuring that key managerial and technical staff understand and accept responsibility for assigned roles and tasks.

Typical Microcomputer Uses For Key Management Tasks	Microcomputer Products Corresponding to Various Uses
A1. Store, process, and analyze data on characteristics of various institutions and individuals involved in and affected by the development activity.	A1a. Narrative profiles and diagrams of organizational structure and individual skills and competencies.
A2. Store, process, and analyze personnel, contracting, procurement, training, and procedural data including data bank of job descriptions, candidates, and staff characteristics.	A2a. Descriptive lists of key information, e.g., available staff and contractor characteristics.
B1. Store, process, and analyze current and project workloads of various units and individuals to ensure a proper balance and realistic allocation of responsibility and authority.	B1a. Descriptive and comparative statistics. B1b. Workload projections.
C1. Store formats and specifications for negotiating and making responsibility assignments for various tasks.	C1a. Blank responsibility charts. C1b. Narrative instructions for negotiating roles, and responsibilities.
C2. Provide a visual display of responsibility assignments to key actors for their reaction, modification, and timely agreement.	C2a. Negotiated responsibility charts.
D1. Provide quick means whereby involved personnel can list and visually view responsibility assignment preferences and decisions.	D1a. Modified responsibility charts accompanied by explanatory text.

Generic Management Functions Associated with Successful Management of Development Projects and Institutions	Management Tasks Related to the Generic Management Functions
IV. Contextually appropriate directive and control mechanisms (including incentives and sanctions) for executing tasks in accordance with plans.	A. Plan and control work activities according to negotiated plans.
	B. Maintain programmatic and financial records, and produce summary reports for interested government/ business, donor agency, and contract personnel.
	C. Conduct internal activity reviews and evaluations assess current and projected status and recommend improvement/ major modifications to design and implementation.
	D. Employ an appropriate work execution process adapted to organizational and individual values and constraints.

Typical Microcomputer Uses For Key Management Tasks	Microcomputer Products Corresponding to Various Uses
A1. Store and maintain information on procedures and specifications for activating development efforts including staffing, contracting, training, and inducements/sanctions.	A1a. Narrative text of procedures. A1b. Various regulations, formats and criteria for specifications.
A2. Prepare and edit directives, memoranda of understanding, and other work execution documents.	A2a. Policy directives. A2b. Action memoranda.
B1. Document and file decisions and actions taken.	B1a. Narrative descriptions of implementation action.
B2. Record and maintain file on actual expenditures, program activities, and observed results.	B2a. Narrative descriptions. B2b. Cost and expenditure data. B2c. Activity data. B2d. Time use data.
B3. Prepare summary reports of program status using standardized formats.	B3a. Narrative and numeric reports.
C1. Provide up-to-date accounts of program status and supplementary analytical information useful in decision making.	C1a. Special narrative and statistical reports.
C2. Permit rapid forecasts and projections of personnel workloads, cash flows, inventory, and other execution actions.	C2a. Program and financial analyses and projections.
D1. Provide a fast and reliable means for documenting actions and results—both individually and in team meetings.	D1a. Narrative accounts of rationale for and actual decisions taken.
D2. Store procedures for information use and dissemination.	D2a. Narrative text of procedures.

Generic Management Functions Associated with Successful Management of Development Projects and Institutions	Management Tasks Related to the Generic Management Functions
V. Suitable monitoring, evaluation, and adaptive learning mechanisms for assessing progress and adapting to changes and lessons learned in a flexible and timely manner.	A. Identify information needs, sources of data, and means for collection for all development activities and important external conditions.
	B. Monitor program progress, unexpected changes in external conditions and key lessons learned relative to plans, and analyze/reassess plans based on this information.
	C. Explore implications of alternative action strategies and undertake calculations of benefits, feasibility, and costs associated with actual and potential changes.
	D. Employ an appropriate process for assuring that relevant actors receive and understand high-quality feedback--both positive and negative--on a timely basis.

Typical Microcomputer Uses For Key Management Tasks	Microcomputer Products Corresponding to Various Uses
A1. Create files of baseline information of programs to be monitored by cost, activity products, objectives and key external conditions.	A1a. Baseline files by geographical area, functional category, target group, etc. A1b. Baseline descriptive statistics and tables.
A2. Store and maintain formats and specifications for data collection and processing procedures and sources.	A2a. Narrative data collection procedures, guidelines, and formats.
B1. Store planned accounts of resource use, activity, and results and compare against actual progress over time.	B1a. Periodic status reports of planned versus actual progress—text and graphics. B1b. Special reports on problem areas or new opportunities.
B2. File, maintain and analyze descriptive accounts, program changes, lessons learned, and unexpected events over time.	B2a. Narrative descriptions. B2b. Programmatic and financial analyses.
C1. Store data for, and assist in pursuing, a series of "what if" scenarios associated with changes in the initial program plans.	C1a. Statistical analyses of costs and benefits associated with alternative action strategies.
D1. Store and maintain formats and specifications for a program's monitoring and reporting system.	D1a. Blank formats for use in monitoring and reporting. D1b. Narrative description of monitoring procedures.
D2. Provide text and visual displays of current status to key development program actors.	D2a. Visual displays and hard copy of planned versus actual progress.

THE MANAGERIAL APPEAL OF MICROCOMPUTERS

Microcomputers are appealing to managers for several interrelated reasons. First, they represent a new technology that is unique in its ability to "work the way you do." Second, initial development applications have yielded encouraging results. As preliminary field survey data indicate, the management of development projects and institutions presents a variety of ready-made opportunities for using the microcomputer in a cost-effective manner.

Microcomputers have also been promoted as personal learning aids. In our international travels we find that many development personnel are purchasing microcomputers for their learning value in the family, and subsequently discover their utility for work-related activities. Finally, and maybe most importantly, the interest in microcomputers has been stimulated by low cost, high mobility, and small size. Current trends indicate that prices and size are declining while reliability, power, and versatility continue to increase.

Thus, to the busy and committed development manager the microcomputer has a strong personal appeal. While the evidence of microcomputer costs, feasibility, and benefits in developing countries is not exclusively supportive, there is substantial reason to believe that microcomputers are able to further improve development management. The most obvious improvements occur when microcomputers perform the routine, tedious, and time-consuming tasks associated with accounting, reporting, and filing. In this area, microcomputers can provide an alternative to hiring additional staff--an option that must be thoroughly considered in each project situation.

For example, managers can use a microcomputer to quickly prepare memos, complete work plans, and construct budgets, thus releasing technical and administrative staff to assume additional responsibility for guiding, monitoring, and reporting on program design and implementation. Middle- and top-level managers' time can be freed by using the microcomputer for data manipulation, analyses, visual display preparation, document revision, file searching and merging, inventory control, personnel appraisals, and financial management. The time saved can be used productively to consider new opportunities and options to improve decision making. It is likely that the appeal of microcomputers will continue to expand in the light of decreasing public resources, increasing pressures for demonstrable development activity, and the active promotion of even more integrated and user-friendly microcomputer technology.

In contrast to mainframe computers which have had limited impact on management and managers in developing countries, microcomputers have several attractive attributes. To summarize, they:

o   are easier to comprehend and decisively more friendly
     to use;

o   are readily available throughout most of the world;

o   are more reliable and are constructed in a modular
    fashion that facilitates repair and maintenance;

o   have substantial versatility and power in their
    applications including the ability to network with
    other microcomputers and larger computer systems;

o   are relatively inexpensive (ranging from $1,000 to
    $5,000) for a complete hardware and software system.

In the last few years the microcomputer has increased in popularity
over mini and mainframe computers. The microcomputer, however, also
has a number of limitations as a management tool. If precautions are
not taken in acquiring and using microcomputers, these limitations may
outstrip their benefits. A summary of the major strengths and limitations of microcomputers, based on developing country experience to
date, is presented in Chapter IV.

CHAPTER II
Hardware and Software:
Keys to User-Friendliness

A microcomputer system is composed of several pieces of electronic equipment (the hardware) which operate by means of various programs (the software) to perform specific information processing tasks within an organizational or human setting.

In this chapter we will consider the importance of user-friendliness and then look at some of the attributes of hardware and software. In Chapter III the organizational dimensions are considered.

THE IMPORTANCE OF USER-FRIENDLINESS IN MICROCOMPUTER SYSTEMS

The concept of user-friendliness is revolutionizing the use of microcomputers: technicians and highly trained operators are no longer required to operate a computer. Anyone, with some appropriate instruction, using packaged software (software developed to perform specific tasks) can quickly learn to use a microcomputer.

Originally, to understand the computer, one had to be fluent in a programming language (e.g., FORTRAN) or an application language (e.g., SPSS) with its own syntax and structure. This requirement isolated all but a handful of initiates from computer use and still partially restricts perceived and actual accessibility to large computers. This is not typically the case with the microcomputer. Because of the user-friendliness designed into the software, people with relatively little training can instruct the microcomputer to do what they want it to do. This change is vitally important--the microcomputer is programmed to speak the user's language.

Of equal importance is the user-friendliness of the hardware. While care is required, the antiseptic conditions needed to sustain the large mainframes are no longer necessary. Nor does a certified technician stand between you and the equipment. You, not the technician, run the program. Moreover, the degree of interaction between the components and the user makes the use of the system remarkably simple. You merely have to connect a cable to a particular circuit board to connect the printer. With many models, if you want to add more memory, you simply buy another circuit board and install it easily.

Structured Flexibility

In a period of an hour, and with minimal instruction, it is now commonplace to use a new software program to prepare written documents, do simple accounting of expenditures, and plan activities and

schedules. User-friendly software programs and their accompanying
documentation provide an overall framework that allows you to carry out
a particular task. The program is structured to help you make choices
and enter data in the correct format for storage and processing.

Many software programs, such as the spreadsheets now available, have
the flexibility to allow you to handle peculiarities of your own work
and setting. Indeed, many software programs are highly adaptable and
redefinable within the overall structure of the program. A spreadsheet
program can be an inventory sheet or an accounts payable, a database
can be a client listing or a sophisticated accounting program. You,
the user, can select numerous program options to suit your own needs.

This combined structure and flexibility of software programs, which we
refer to as "structured-flexibility," allows users at different levels
of expertise and time availability to appreciate the same software
packages.

<u>Skill Levels of Microcomputer Users</u>

The concept of user-friendliness is a relative one. It depends in part
on skill levels of the potential user. Other things being equal, the
more skilled you are in microcomputer system acquisition and use, the
more friendly a microcomputer will appear to be. These skill levels
can be viewed as follows:

    o   Level 1: Persons who enter data on a routine basis in a
user-friendly packaged program, where data have been pre-coded.
Persons who know how to use manuals to find out what is wrong with the
equipment, but never assemble, maintain, or repair the equipment;

    o   Level 2: Managers who use the data for a user-friendly program
that meets well-defined and understood management needs. Persons who
have some understanding of the hardware, can replace boards and do
routine maintenance;

    o   Level 3: Persons who can deal with problems that are too
difficult or time-consuming for the manager to handle in a program that
is user-friendly and well suited to the application. Persons more
sophisticated in their ability to troubleshoot problems and who can
install a system; and

    o   Level 4: Persons who can make decisions on which software
programs to use, how to customize them, and how to create tailor-made
programs. Persons who are also able to design systems, adapting both
the hardware and software to particular management needs. They are
thus skilled technicians as well as programmers.

An individual's skill level with user-friendly microcomputer systems
will determine how much use will be made of the equipment's capabilities. To the extent that the user is more knowledgeable, the
flexibility of user-friendly programs expands. This in no way

minimizes the novice's ability to use a software program to fit a
particular application to do a particular job. The next step must be
to examine the kinds of available hardware and software in order to
further assess what you and a microcomputer can accomplish together.

USER-FRIENDLY MICROCOMPUTER HARDWARE

The hardware of a microcomputer is made up of several components--a
keyboard, a central processing unit, memory, a monitor, disk drives,
and a printer.   A keyboard is used to enter data and information into
the computer. The monitor shows what is being or has been entered. A
printer produces a copy of the work on paper. Processing takes place
and information is electronically stored in the central memory and in
the storage devices such as diskettes. These components can be configured together or can be purchased separately (see Figure 3). Here
we will discuss each of these components in some detail.

THE MONITOR: The monitor is the TV-like screen used to display the information that is being input into the computer. On the monitor you not only see what you are doing and the changes that you are making while you work, but you also receive information and directions from the computer itself. It is the visual communication link between the central processing unit (CPU) and you.

THE CENTRAL PROCESSING UNIT: The central processing unit is the "brain" of the microcomputer where the information is processed. The CPU is the main information link for all of the internal components of the computer that contain the operating system. The CPU is not a single piece of equipment but a collection of circuit boards and wires that serve to route information that comes in through the keyboard, transmit the information to appropriate components, and make needed computations. All peripheral equipment must be linked to the CPU so that information is processed and transmitted.

THE KEYBOARD: A microcomputer keyboard is much like a typewriter keyboard, but there are a number of additional keys for additional functions. There are either two or three sets of keys. The large set contains, in addition to all of the regular typewriting keys, an escape key and a control key. Depending on the manufacturer, you will have a number keypad containing the cursor keys, or the cursor keys will be included with the large set. Some manufacturers, such as IBM, provide special programmable function keys to access special commands.

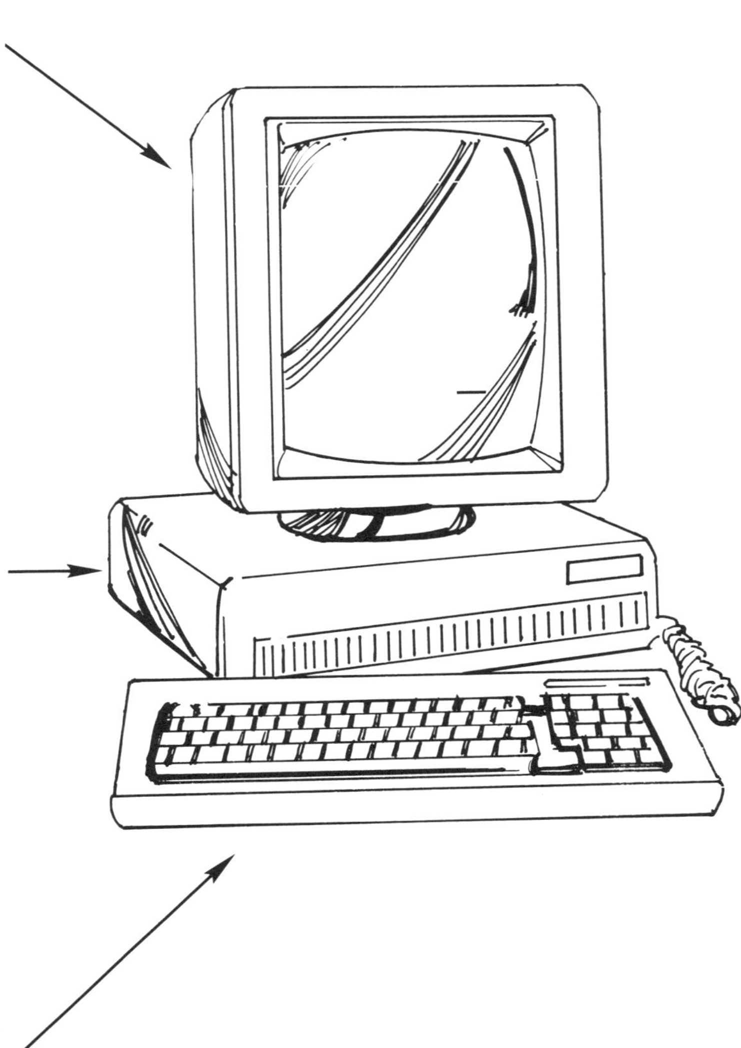

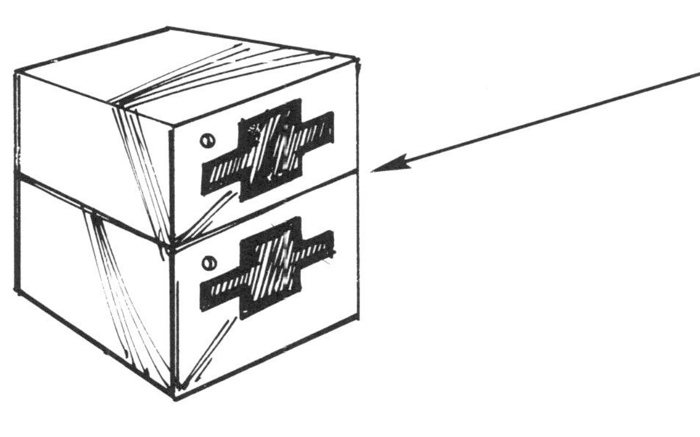

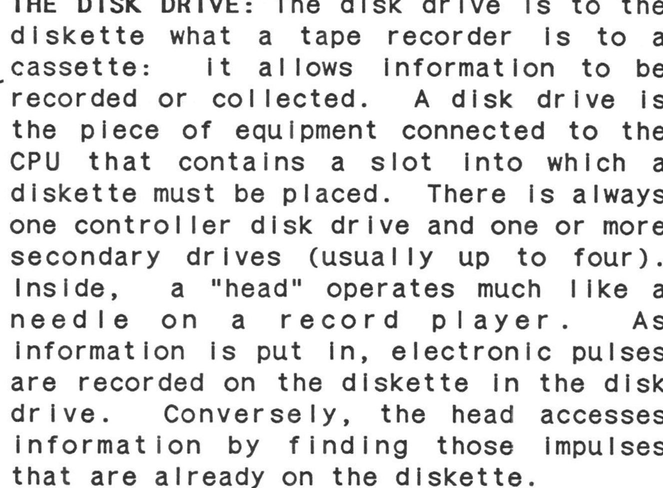

THE DISK DRIVE: The disk drive is to the diskette what a tape recorder is to a cassette: it allows information to be recorded or collected. A disk drive is the piece of equipment connected to the CPU that contains a slot into which a diskette must be placed. There is always one controller disk drive and one or more secondary drives (usually up to four). Inside, a "head" operates much like a needle on a record player. As information is put in, electronic pulses are recorded on the diskette in the disk drive. Conversely, the head accesses information by finding those impulses that are already on the diskette.

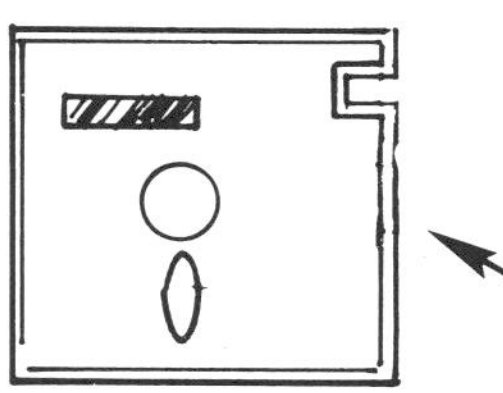

THE DISKETTE: The diskettes, or disks, are round, plastic "records" encased in protective square cardboard coverings. There is an opening that, when inserted into the disk drive, touches the head from the drive that is receiving information from or transmitting information to the CPU. The electronic impulses, equalling characters, are thus stored on the diskette.

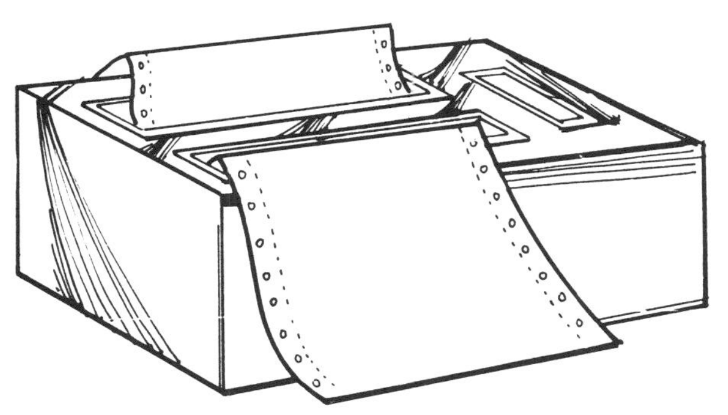

THE PRINTER: The printer is also attached to the CPU and is connected through a cable and the operating system software. Printers are necessary for most development work, but depending on the function, different kinds are required. Dot-matrix printers are typically used for making charts and tables. Letter quality printers give the letter quality type of a typewriter.

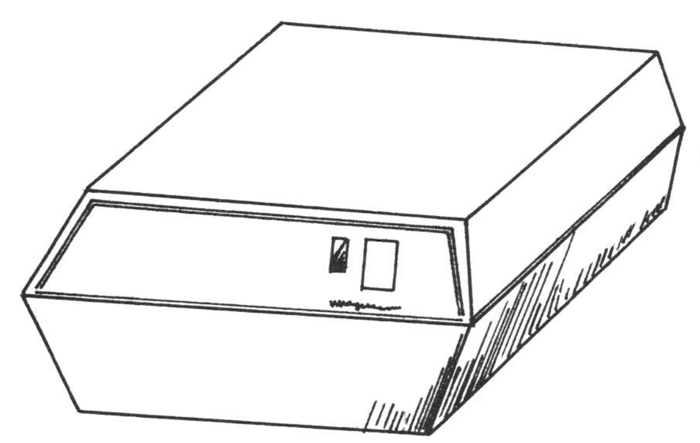

THE UPS OR STABILIZER: The UPS is recommended for developing country situations as it stabilizes electrical current before it reaches the computer. In case of black or brown-outs, the battery-operated UPS will keep the computer running long enough to avoid damage.

Central Processing Unit

The main unit of the computer usually contains the central processing
unit (commonly referred to as the CPU) and internal working memory.
The central processing unit performs the arithmetic calculations and
logical operations on the data as instructed by programs held within
memory. The CPU physically initiates and directs the flow of data in
the main unit, does the needed calculations, comparisons, and analyses.
It does this in step-by-step conformance with a predetermined procedure
called a "program." These programs are contained either permanently in
memory or are accessible on disks, magnetic tapes, or some other
external means.

The central processing unit can exist separately (see Figure 3) or be
combined as a single unit with the keyboard, and/or monitor, and/or
disk drives. There are reasons why one configuration would be preferable over the other. For example, when you need to attach a monitor
and disk drive to make a complete system, it is easier to move around
several smaller components; repairs and maintenance are easier too,
since a problem can be isolated by trying different subsections. In a
central unit with everything built in, you lose some maintenance
flexibility.

Correctly isolating hardware problems can be important in developing
countries. If you have to send the item away for repair, it is often
convenient to send only the sub-unit needing repair instead of the
entire unit. The savings could be considerable.

The Keyboard

The keyboard of a microcomputer is much like that of a typewriter. It
is sometimes (as on the Apple II) attached to the CPU. The microcomputer keyboard is wider than a typewriter keyboard because it has
several extra keys for a number of additional functions. The typewriter
normally has 88 keys, while the microcomputer has at least 94 on the
main keyboard. Further, some microcomputer keyboards have three sets
of keys, the large set, the number pad and the function keys. The
large set contains the typewriter keys, the escape key (that lets you
escape from a command you have given the computer), the control key
(that allows you to change a regular typewriter key into a command key
by pressing it in conjunction with that key), and other keys with
specific functions. The number pad is usually found to the right and
is sometimes combined with the cursor keys (the arrows that help you
move around the monitor screen). On some key pads, the keys are
programmable and on others there is a third set of function keys to
program according to individual needs for particular software programs.

Memory

The microcomputer stores information either inside the central unit
and/or externally. Because the internal storage capacity of today's

microcomputer is usually inadequate as permanent storage, having a device for permanent external storage is crucial. Diskettes are one way to provide this permanent data storage capability.

Internal storage is generally classified as ROM and RAM. ROM, "Read Only Memory", contains permanent information and refers to internal computer programs that the microcomputer utilizes to set itself up every time you use it. This includes getting ready to accept information from you, reading files when requested, etc. RAM stands for "Random Access Memory," which is that part of memory you can use to load programs and store data for immediate access and reference. RAM is made up of integrated circuit chips. Each chip has a capacity that is measured in "K" bits of data. "K" stands for kilo, but don't be deceived, when applied to computers, that means 1024 bits. Thus, a 16K RAM chip has a capacity of 16 x 1024 bits. A byte consists of eight bits; computer capacity is measured in "K" bytes of internal memory. There are several 8 bit microcomputers on the market, but 16 and 32 bit machines are standard.

Most microcomputers being used in development projects have 64K or 256K bytes of RAM storage--the amount of memory needed for most packaged software presently used in development. It is sometimes difficult to add memory to a 64K computer, but most 256K computers are built so that you can add up to 640K of additional memory for approximately $20 per 64K.

Note: The amount of RAM determines what software programs you can run, not how much information you can store. Some programs (WordStar) require 64K of RAM to process data, some (Symphony) require 640K. The amount of data you can store depends on the disk drive or storage device chosen.

<u>Storage Devices</u>

<u>Disk Drives</u>: The disk drive is the piece of equipment that transfers information coming from the CPU onto a diskette or accesses information that is already on a diskette. After a diskette is placed in a disk drive, the drive stores information electronically on it--whether it is a record-type "floppy" disk or a hard disk. Generally, the manu- facturer of a microcomputer makes its own drives (IBM drives for an IBM computer) but there are many other reputable drive manufacturers and it is not unusual to "swap" drives from one computer to another after ascertaining their compatibility.

<u>Floppy Disks</u>: Diskettes are used to store computer information exter- nally. There are three sizes: the 3 inch, the 5 1/4 inch, and the 8 inch. How much a diskette will hold depends on the type of disk format and density (single or double), type of drive used, and whether you can use both sides of the floppy disk. Once a diskette is inserted into a disk drive you can access data/information stored on it by typing certain commands on the keyboard. You can also add, delete, or change information based on your interaction with the central processing unit.

The standard size for most microcomputers in the field is 5 1/4 inch. The typical 5 1/4 inch disk is double sided and double density, which gives you about 360K of storage space per diskette. Consider 100K equivalent to approximately 65 pages of text. Eight inch diskettes generally store more information than the smaller disks. Their drives look similar to the smaller disk drives and function the same way. Besides having more storage capacity per diskette, 8 inch diskettes allow faster access to the information. This can be important if you require frequent searches for special information across large data bases.

Technology is changing rapidly in disk storage capacity. There are now three inch disks on the market that store more information than the standard 5 1/4 inch disks. There are also multiple density 5 1/4 inch disks storing as much as several hard drives on the market.

Hard Disks: Hard disks, fixed disks and Winchester drives are all the same thing. They store very large amounts of information and are very fast. The hard disk is made of high-grade aluminum and cannot be removed from your computer (except for maintenance). Hard drives eliminate the need for changing floppy disks whenever you want to switch to another software program--everything is installed on the high capacity drive. Your need for a hard disk drive depends on your data base and other requirements.

The capacity of a hard disk is measured in megabytes (one million bytes). The standard at this time is the ten megabyte internal drive such as in the Kaypro 10 or the IBM XT, but once again technology is giving us more storage capacity--from five megabytes to 120 megabytes at this time.

External Hard Drives: These are portable units that attach to your microcomputer to expand the original storage. They are identical to the internal hard disks described above, but are modular and can be attached to different computers. Special boards must be installed in your computer before an external hard drive can be attached.

Cartridge Disks: Removable cartridge disks are a cross between hard and floppy disks. Imagine removing the internal hard disk from the computer and inserting it in a plastic case similar to the cardboard case of the floppy. This allows you to have the large storage capacity of the hard drive in a cartridge that can be removed and stored for back-up purposes, or you can have one high capacity cartridge for each project.

Tape: One of the problems with large capacity drives, either internal, external, or cartridge, is that in order to make back-up copies of your important data, you find yourself filling up hundreds of floppy disks in a time-consuming process. Cartridge tapes (or tape streamers) allow you to make mirror images on tape of the contents of your hard drive quickly and efficiently.

<u>Some Storage Considerations</u>

A wide variety of data storage equipment is available, and even more
sophisticated equipment is being marketed. The specific applicability
of this new equipment to development projects remains to be seen. When
designing your system you should give close consideration to what is
presently used in the field. Investigate thoroughly before purchasing a
hard disk system or a system that is dependent on new state-of-the-art
technology. Lack of field testing is a major reason to avoid taking
the newest trends in microcomputer technology to a development setting.

For the average development project, the size of the database or
spreadsheet program can be fairly easily determined and thus, the type
of disk drives properly selected. Floppy disk systems are more than
adequate for most field work, but larger projects may require higher
capacity storage.

The cost of a hard disk or cartridge system is currently $500 to $700
more than that of a floppy-based microcomputer and can provide a cost
effective alternative to floppies. Keep in mind that they are more
sensitive to harsh environments than their floppy counterparts. As you
become more dependent on your computer system you will want to have
access to trained maintenance and repair technicians and spare parts.
Backing up a hard drive requires some consideration--if you are going
to back up to floppy disks, be prepared to spend some time doing it.
If you want to back up to tapes or cartridges, that is another cost
consideration.

Generally, a project user has a 5 1/4 or 8 inch disk drive system with
two to four disk drives and a CPU with 64K or 256K of RAM storage. Two
disk drives seem to be the minimum required; four are more than adequate for a small microcomputer system used in a development project
situation. Since almost any system can be "upgraded" in the future,
start with what is necessary to run the software you have chosen for
your present needs. You can expand in the future.

<u>Operating Systems and Languages</u>

Each microcomputer has an internal operating system--a set of programs
that supports the central processing unit in performing any operation.
An operating system contains the programs for running hardware peripherals (the printer, the monitor, etc.), system start-up (boot)
programs, and general system utility programs (sorting, error messages,
delete, run, etc.).

Operating systems differ among microcomputer companies and, generally,
are hardware specific, such as Apple DOS, Hewlett Packard and Wang.
Generally these systems are incompatible. There is one operating
system considered the standard, however, and most manufacturers include
the capability of running this operating system in their microcomputer.
It is the IBM-compatible operating system, known as MS or PC DOS.

A variety of languages can be used to communicate both within the microcomputer and between the user and the microcomputer. "Language" is used here as in ordinary parlance, to mean some logical system for using a standard set of symbols to translate data into information. For example, whenever the word "print" is used, the microcomputer will print the next statement during execution. The highest level language refers to the one that communicates between the program and the microcomputer CPU; and is the one in which the software is written. This language is often some form of the BASIC language.

The microcomputer reacts to you and responds in a low-level application language--your everyday language. The important point, to underscore the user-friendly concept, is that packaged software programs can communicate with you in your language. You do not have to learn BASIC or any other high-level language to use packaged software programs.

Video Monitors

A video monitor is necessary so that you can see what you are doing with your computer. The standard monitor has been some combination of black, white, and/or grey. However, the green or amber screens are often preferred if one person will be working at the machine for several consecutive hours. Eye strain (especially during the first few weeks/months of use) is reduced with amber and green screen models.

A color monitor is mainly needed for the use of graphics: seeing various charts or graphs plotted in multiple colors brings the information to life and makes the data speak. But a color monitor is not particularly easy to work with for regular data entry because of poor resolution of the image. Eye strain is often greater with a color monitor than with amber, green, or black and white screen models.

Printers

The printer is generally a separate unit or component. The most common printers are the dot matrix impact, non-impact, and the letter quality models. Most printers are available in "short" carriage for 8 1/2 by 11 inch paper and "wide" carriage for 230 column paper.

Dot Matrix: The least expensive output printer is the dot matrix impact. These printers use a print head that creates each character by printing a number of dots. Usually there are several qualities of print. "Draft" quality is the fastest: the characters are not quite complete, nor do they look like typed script. "Correspondence" or "near letter" quality uses more dots to create each character, which slows the printing speed but improves the readability. Depending on your word processing program, most dot matrix printers enlarge the print or allow you to create a variety of other special characters. If you are interested in doing graphics, a dot matrix printer is a necessity.

The dot matrix is preferred in most development settings for doing drafts and graphic work. It is the general workhorse, the least expensive and the most dependable printer, and usually is equipped with tractor feed for inexpensive continuous form computer paper.

<u>Non-Impact Printers</u>: The principal virtue of non-impact printers is that they are very fast and quiet. Of those used in development projects, the laser printer and the ink-jet are most popular.

     o   <u>Laser</u> The laser printer is basically a cross between a standard office copier and a dot matrix printer. Capable of printing in a variety of type styles and fonts and with tremendous graphics capability, laser printing rivals typesetting for clean flexible manuscript production.

     o   <u>Ink-Jet</u> Ink-jet printers are similar to dot matrix printers in speed and resolution, but run much more quietly. They print through a process of spraying drops of liquid ink onto paper with enough force to penetrate the paper fibers. Although most manufacturers will say ink-jet printers work well with plain paper, a special chemically treated paper greatly improves print quality. These printers are usually light and, thus, quite portable.

<u>Letter Quality Printers</u>: Letter quality printers come in two types--daisywheel and thimble. Although often the most expensive printers, they produce a print character comparable to that of a fine electric typewriter. The daisywheels or thimbles come in a variety of type faces and languages, but it is wise to check availability before buying a letter quality printer for use with an obscure typeface or language.

<u>Modems</u>

Modems allow microcomputers to communicate via telephone. The modem translates digital signals (which computers use for communication) to analog signals (which telephones use for communication) at the sender's location and reverses the translation at the receiver's location. Thus, when two computers are connected through modems they can communicate with each other and access data.

Essentially there are two standards for modems: Bell in the United States and CCITT (Telegraph and Telephone Consultative Committee) in the rest of the world. Because of this difference in frequency, a CCITT system will not work in the United States and the Bell System will not work anywhere but the United States. Even if they are running at the same software, these two systems will not be able to communicate. The only way to effectively communicate internationally is to have a modem that operates on both the Bell and the CCITT standards.

The telephone system in most developing countries is unreliable and does not generally provide an environment conducive to modem interfacing. In countries where the system is reliable, it is possible to access mainframe databases and share information between microcomputers located at different sites. This communication could be valuable, for instance, for sharing program and financial information between regional offices and central offices. Furthermore, a modem allows individuals to communicate via the microcomputer in the same way they do by telephone--except in written words. Appendix B provides a description of CARINET, a computer conferencing network dedicated to the transfer of technology to the developing world.

Local Area Networks

As development organizations become more familiar with the use of microcomputers, they are beginning to realize that their management capability can be enhanced further by installing Local Area Networks (LANs)--linking two or more computers to allow access to programs on either computer. These multi-user systems generally consist of a file-server (usually a computer with a hard disk drive and large storage capacity) connected to other less expensive and less powerful computer(s). The peripheral computers can access programs on the file server, usually for data entry. Because networking requires steady power and enhanced technical expertise, it is not yet used extensively in developing country settings. Technological advances are making multi-user systems more fault tolerant and user-friendly, and we feel that it is a logical "next step" for experienced microcomputer users.

Single Unit Computers

Transportable, portable and laptop computers are single unit machines that are generally very small and powerful. Fitting inside an attache-sized case, they travel well and contain monitor, disk drives, CPU, keyboard and power supply in one unit. Information can be printed directly from laptops or downloaded to microcomputer for manipulation. Repair is easy since they weigh very little and can be sent or carried to a maintenance facility. Although it is not possible to troubleshoot by isolating subsections as with modular units, several very good hardware diagnostic software packages are available to help the user with maintenance and diagnosis.

There are many system configuration options. In Table 2 we summarize the various hardware components, their uses, and their advantages and disadvantages.

Table 2   Microcomputer Hardware Components, Uses, Pros and Cons

Component	Use	Pros	Cons
ENTIRE SYSTEM	Processing information		
--Configured together		Portability of entire unit	Hard to isolate problems
--Configured separately		Easier to maintain, isolate problems	Lack of portability of whole system
<u>Central Processing Unit/Internal Memory</u>	Memory; stores information; processes data	Easy to add memory in most computers*	
<u>Keyboard</u>	Keys give commands to CPU		Angle of key board; loca-tion of keys
<u>Disk Drive</u>	Allows storage and retrieval of information from disks		
--Only one		External storage; less expensive	Diskettes must be be changed frequently
--More than one		Program and data can be in separate drives;	More expensive

* While it is often possible to add to internal memory, an important consideration is the extent to which the additional memory can be integrated.

Table 2 (Continued)

Component	Use	Pros	Cons
<u>Diskettes</u>	Store information		
3 inch		Small; more storage than 5 1/4	Not common in field
5 1/4 inch		Standard in development settings	
8 inch		Bigger, faster, more storage	Costs more than 5 1/4
Hard disk		Increased storage	Expensive; needs skilled repair
Cartridge		Large storage; can move easily between computers	Still testing in the field
<u>Monitors</u>			
Green screen	View image of work	Eye strain reduced	
Amber screen	View image of work	Least eye strain	Somewhat more costly
Color	View image of work in color, graphics; games	Makes graphics alive	Resolution poor for word/data processing

Microcomputer Hardware Components, Uses, Pros, and Cons

Component	Use	Pros	Cons
<u>Printers</u>			
Dot matrix	General; graphics	Least expensive; fast	Not letter quality
Non-Impact	General; graphics	Fast; quiet; versatile	Expensive paper; not tested in field
Letter Quality	Letters; reports	Excellent print quality; inexpensive paper	Limited graphics; slow
<u>Modem</u>	Allows inter-communication/ interfacing with other systems	Inexpensive communication	Needs com-patible functional phone system
<u>LANs</u>	Connecting of two or more computers	More computing power; access to programs and storage on linked computers	Expensive; untested in field; needs good technical support
<u>Lap-tops</u>	Processing information	Small; travel easily; inexpensive	Need special add-ons for field use

The hardware components of a microcomputer system--including size, physical configuration and computing power--establish the boundaries of the potential usefulness of a microcomputer. The type of hardware influences the portability of the system, the time and expertise required to install and ready the system for operation, and the ease of maintenance and repair.

The hardware also determines the maximum computing power available to a user and the speed at which information processing tasks can be performed. Thus, the selection of a keyboard, monitor, CPU, disk drives, and printer for use in a developing country is an important decision. The availability of other computers, technicians, paper and other accessories are basic to any decision. However, in all cases, the final decision depends on an analysis of your particular needs and skill level with microcomputer technology. A detailed discussion of needs assessment follows in Chapter III.

USER-FRIENDLY MICROCOMPUTER SOFTWARE

The sets of procedures and rules that instruct the computer how to perform particular tasks are the software programs. These programs are stored on diskettes or are part of the memory of the central processing unit. The hardware is useless without them. Further, the software programs define the types of applications you can perform, (although the job requirements will define the software you will want). Using several different software programs, one computer can perform various functions: report writing, statistical analysis, project planning.

Software programs are the key to the kind of microcomputer you need. When assessing your need for a microcomputer you must first determine what tasks you need the system to do, and the software that can do them. Then decide what kind of hardware to buy. Each software program, in effect, turns the microcomputer into a special-purpose tool. There are two kinds of software, operating systems and ap-plications software.

Operating Systems

The operating system is typically built into the hardware components of a microcomputer and may provide scheduling, debugging (removing mistakes), input/output control, compilation, storage assignment, data management, and related functions. (Apple DOS, MS and PC DOS, and CP/M are examples of operating systems.) Although the operating system is built into memory of the CPU, operating system software is needed to control the execution of other computer programs and internal func-tions. In some microcomputers the operating system software must be placed in the disk drive before programs can be run. In others this is not necessary. It is also the operating system software that you modify to accommodate peripheral equipment.

Many microcomputers are capable of handling more than one operating
system. For example, there are hardware add-ons that change an Apple
system so that it is capable of running IBM programs. Although a
program that is written for one operating system will not run on
another, there are utility programs available to allow the transfer of
data files from one operating system to another.

APPLICATIONS SOFTWARE

Applications software programs refer to individual software packages
that instruct the microcomputer to perform specific tasks such as word
processing, calculations, etc. "Software" commonly means applications
software. In this guide we emphasize "packaged" applications software
programs.

Types of Software: Custom versus Packaged

There are two basic kinds of applications software: custom and
packaged. Custom software is usually designed for a specific application when there is no packaged software available to do the job. An
example of custom-designed software is the series of agricultural
software packages catalogued by J. Robert Strain at the University of
Florida (see Bibliography). A "packaged" software program (such as an
accounting system) is used in a variety of ways by a variety of users.
You may create your own custom accounting system (many people do), or
you may use a packaged software program, created to be used by many
organizations for many needs.

Custom software programs can be costly and time-consuming to produce.
For this reason alone you should explore what packaged software exists
before reinventing the wheel. Packaged software programs usually were
developed to meet specific applications or needs. More are becoming
available every day.

Characteristics of User-Friendly Software

Several features characterize a computer program as user-friendly;
Assuming the program is written in your speaking or reading language,
it should:

   o   be menu-driven;

   o   have high quality error trapping capabilities; and

   o   have associated documentation that is easy to read and
       understand.

Menu-driven Formats: Menu-driven formats have improved the quality of
many software programs. The user sees a list of operations on the
screen and chooses one by pressing the key that is specified. The
computer then, automatically, sets itself up to perform that function

and provides the user with the information needed to proceed to the next step.

A menu-driven software program is controlled, ordered, and organized by a list of options (commands) that contains sub-lists as needed. An example of a main menu might be:

<u>Example of a Main Menu</u>

E — Edit a document
H — Help with a problem
P — Print a document
S — Check spelling
T — Teach the program

<u>Error Trapping</u>: A good user-friendly software program has built-in stops and whistles that help you understand how to use the program and alert you to possible mistakes.

For example: If you try to name a file with a name that already exists, the program gives the message: FILE EXISTS

The concept of "error trapping" is important. Once you are using a program, it is possible to lose information; a good user-friendly program will have built-in safeguards to reduce these possibilities. Another example is a program that prevents accidentally deleting information: each time you give the "delete file" command, it asks, "ARE YOU SURE YOU WANT TO DELETE THIS FILE?" This kind of safeguard makes software programs user-friendly.

Good menus are written in clear language. The options represent a clear logic and have a basic relation to the machine's functions. In this way, users always know exactly where they are within the program. The ability to move to the next lower or higher order menu within the program is another example of user-friendly programming.

<u>Easy-to-Understand Documentation</u>: User-friendly documentation generally meets several standards; the most important are listed below. The manual and program:

o   are clear, easy to use and understand, and well
     indexed;

o   list each error message that may appear and how to
     interpret it;

o   provide as many examples as necessary to demonstrate
     each of the possible optional uses of each command
     within each menu;

o   have ability to cross-reference any key word within the
     documentation;

o   provide a back-up copy of the program and a policy for
     getting additional copies in case of damage;

o   offer a built-in tutorial program for any and all uses
     of the program;

o   have a built-in "help" command for assistance within
     the   program while using it and for retrieving
     information on using the various program commands.

Most companies offer a technical assistance service over the telephone.
This service may be of little value in your field placement, however,
so the more familiar you are with the software you are going to use,
the better. It is important to stress that no matter how user-friendly
the software, there will always be problems understanding the manual
and the options until you become familiar with at least one computer
program and with the structure of menu-driven software in general.

<u>Common Types of Applications Software Programs</u>

There are many packaged software programs that are useful in
development projects and institutions. Each has a wide range of
applications. The three most commonly used are:

o   **Electronic Spreadsheets:** powerful programs to enter
     values into a matrix-like grid and define their
     interrelation for making projections and testing
     assumptions;

o   **Word Processing:** programs to assist you in the
     preparation of materials and reports;

o   **Database Management:** programs to structure information
     for selective manipulation and retrieval;

Other applications software programs that are useful to development
projects are:

o   **Work Scheduling and Monitoring:** programs that permit
     the listing and comparative assessments of work
     activities over time;

o   **Graphics:** programs for drawing pictures or plots on the
     screen, and transferring drawings to paper;

o   **Statistics and Computations:** programs used to analyze
     and report on various types of data;

o	**Accounting:** programs used to set up and maintain financial records;

o	**Education and Learning:** primarily self-instructional programs; and

o	**Personal Entertainment:** programs for personal enjoyment including action games and puzzles.

Software programs are produced by many different companies; many programs are quite similar in terms of application. In Table 3 we present common applications and trade names for the basic kinds of software useful to development management situations.

Table 3

Common Types of Microcomputer Software,
Special Purpose Software Packages, and
Typical Development Management Applications

Software Category	Common Software	Representative Development Management Application
Database Management Systems	DB Master dBase II dBase III Rbase 5000 CONDOR III	Accounting system, file record keeping, directories, personnel tracking, task/resources tracking, inventory control.
Word Processing	WordStar 2000 Word Perfect Magic Window Microsoft Word Volkswriter Deluxe Apple Writer II Superscribe	Text creation of reports, memos, form or individual letters, editing, indexing, hyphenation, spelling.
Electronic Spreadsheet	Lotus 1-2-3 SuperCalc 3 Multiplan Profit Plan	Calculations, financial planning budgeting, cost-benefit analysis, manpower planning, budget comparisons, simulation, model building.
Statistics and Computation	Daisy Professional SPSS Microstat ABSTAT Linear Programming	Descriptive statistics, regression analysis, analysis of variance, non-parametric analysis, base line data analysis, cause/effect analysis; generates most forms applicable to development projects and institution-strengthening efforts.
Telecommunications	MITE Crosstalk XVI/ Crosstalk 3.0 Modem 7	Via modem, dial phone numbers, log on to remote system automatically, capture and save incoming data, send data and hang up automatically.

**Common Types of Microcomputer Software, Special
Purpose Software Packages, and
Typical Development Management Applications**

Software Category	Common Software	Representative Development Management Application
Integrated Packages	Framework Symphony Open Access Applewerks	Usually combines word processing, spreadsheet, data manager. Can include telecommunications, graphics, and programming languages.
Accounting	Solomon III DAC-EASY IMS Fund System Continental PC-FUND Nonprofit Accounting	Generates monthly summary accounts; ages accounts receivable/payable; creates accounting sheets and income statements.
Work Scheduling and Monitoring Control	Milestone APM Harvard Project Manager	Lists of work activities, allocating resources monitoring accomplishments against planned work targets, management information.
Educational and Personal Development	LOGO PROLOG typing tutors language programs	Logical concepts; systems thinking; foreign and programming languages.
Graphics	Apple Plot Graphic Pak Fastgraph Microsoft Chart	Diagrams, charts, visual display of concepts/ideas.
Personal Entertainment	Sargon III Flight Simulator Zork I, II, III Dragon World	Chess, quiz games, action games

Electronic Spreadsheets: The electronic spreadsheet deserves particular attention. It is a highly flexible tool for worksheet calculations of various types: simulation and model building, financial planning, budgeting, cost-benefit analysis, and quarterly charts of data that require frequent revision or changes. For example, imagine a very large arithmetic table that has fifty columns and approximately 250 rows or about 12,500 "cells." (Column widths can be set to suit your needs.) You can label columns and rows using appropriate headings for your calculations. You can enter data and establish algebraic and arithmetic relationships among cells that are then carried out automatically. It is possible to set up individual tables <u>within</u> the large tables with preset relationships within the smaller tables and between tables. When you enter original data in a blank table, the "answer" cells (connected by a formula) are produced automatically--according to formulas you have entered in them. If you change entries, the "answer cells" will change immediately to conform to the changes.

The earliest electronic spreadsheet on the market was VisiCalc, closely followed by the more versatile SuperCalc and Multiplan. Building on the success of these early spreadsheet programs is Lotus 1-2-3, an extremely advanced spreadsheet that combines the features of an easy-to-use spreadsheet program with graphics and data management functions. At this writing, 1-2-3 is probably the most-used and appreciated program in development work.

Spreadsheets can handle arithmetic functions, present values, exponentials, and internal rates of return. All of these functions can be extremely important for looking at different alternatives or "what if" situations. You can make changes and examine their impact on the rest of the worksheet. For example: "What if the bean crop were increased by 10% while the coffee crop were decreased by 8%?" Once the blank form is set up for a particular framework of calculation, simple entries immediately give full blown tables that give the answers as well as the original entries. Once satisfied with the table on the screen, you can then print it on paper.

An electronic spreadsheet is such a useful management tool that many managers believe that it alone makes the purchase of a microcomputer worthwhile.

Word Processing: Word processing is another commonly used software program in the field. The average manager spends an enormous amount of time writing everything from memos to major reports. Word processing assumes only one thing about users--that they can type. Once the keyboard is mastered, word processing offers new levels of writing productivity and the opportunity to get reports out on time.

Word processing is useful because it saves time. If you normally use a pencil and paper to do a draft and then have a secretary type it, your work time can be cut immensely with a word processing program. You will write and edit a document without having to retype it. You can go to final copy without ever printing the document, working instead with the image on the screen.   Word processing programs have built-in commands for indenting paragraphs, left and right margin justification, footnote location, and aligning numbers in columns.   The word processing program will conduct searches for special words/phrases, move words, readjust lines and text to accommodate deletions, center titles, run various print faces, and hyphenate.

The value of word processing for entering and editing information should be fairly clear. Proofreading time is decreased significantly: if small sections of pages, single words, or lines have been changed after an initial proofreading, then only those changes need to be proofed. Proofreading can be done on the screen, thus eliminating the need for paper copies.   In addition, should your work require an index, production time is shortened considerably by using word processing because the unit can be programmed to locate key words.

The value and utility of a word processing program cannot be overstated.   If your work involves a substantial amount of writing, then give serious thought to getting a word processing program.

Database Management: A database management package is a very powerful program for managers. It allows the user to structure multiple pieces of information in such a way that each can be selectively retrieved, combined, displayed, or printed--even from various microcomputer files. A database management program puts the information pieces together to form a base. Once this is arranged, you can use the information in a variety of ways. You can:

- o   compile lists of meeting attendees by their names, sponsoring institutions, and addresses;

- o   prepare periodic (or special) project and financial reports containing a variety of types of required information;

- o   track project resources and personnel over time in terms of current and cumulative expenditures;

- o   maintain an up-to-date mailing list of important professional contacts and institutions; and

- o   keep track of inventory within a project or institution.

In short, database management programs can be used to construct almost any kind of filing or record keeping and reporting system. They are quite flexible and can be designed according to user needs. What a database management program can do may be clarified by considering the following example.

You have a need to select short-term consultants to perform various
tasks. Over the months you have collected a number of resumes and
bio-data forms on individuals who are familiar with your unit and would
be interested in short-term assignments. Your collection of resumes is
now stuffed into several big files in the office and each time you need
a person you are frustrated when you must go through each file looking
for suitable candidates.

With a database management program you could store the resumes on disk.
You could make a list of consultants, identifying some important characteristics (10 or 15) by which you want them classified and retrieved,
including perhaps skill areas, experience, and language ability. When
resumes deemed worthy of future consideration were received, you could
quickly code each into the database. Thus, when you need a particular
kind of person for a job, you could search the files by salient
characteristics. The microcomputer would then provide a list of all
candidates meeting your basic requirements.

A database management program could also be used to set up and
regularly track project accountability schedules. It would then, upon
your command, sort files by one or several items, do arithmetic
operations, calculate summaries, and print out information in a wide
variety of formats. Almost any size and type of file or information
can be established to store data and retrieve it later.

Setting up a database management system does require putting the
relevant information into the computer. However, this is often less of
a problem than it first appears since information can be input a little
at a time or all at once. In most development efforts it is possible
to input data on a recurrent basis either once a month or once
quarterly. Once the information is put on disk, it is always
available. There are restrictions on the size of the database program
depending on the memory of the microcomputer. You should carefully
examine software before purchasing it to assure yourself that
particular program will indeed meet your needs.

Statistics and Computation Applications: Of applications software used
in development applications, statistical programs are among those most
frequently encountered. They are being used to analyze general
economic and agricultural production data. Statistical packages
perform one or more of the following functions:

   o   Descriptive statistics
   o   Regression
   o   Regression analysis
   o   Analysis of variance
   o   Nonparametric analysis

The commercial packages are able to handle any number of observations and work with between 30 and 80 variables. The more popular programs are SPS, which will interface with SPSS, and MicroStat. In all cases, special programming can be done to allow interfacing with mainframe computers. Specific statistics software programs have been written that are applicable to development projects in particular.

Another commonly used computation package is Linear Programming, a software package that has proved useful in determining optimum feed schedules, herd optimization, crop patterns, and crop distribution.

There are a number of customized software programs that do one or two specific applications such as cattle feeding and herd optimization. (Refer to the list compiled by J. Robert Strain, mentioned previously in this chapter.)

Accounting: Commercial accounting programs come in either single or double entry formats and are able to generate the forms considered necessary for the financial records of any development project. General ledger accounting, monthly summary accounts, aged accounts receivable and payable, and balance sheets and income statements can be utilized.

Work Scheduling and Monitoring: A large and rapidly expanding amount of software exists for cataloging work activities and events, scheduling, allocating scarce resources, and monitoring actual accomplishments against planned work targets. Project monitoring (or critical path analysis) encompasses many common project management techniques as well as management information systems. Many software packages have been tailored to the specific needs of individual project managers.

Graphics: Graphics software represents a powerful category of support programs--ideas and trends can be diagrammed, charted, or pictured. This software permits the entering, creating, and copying of drawings and diagrams, and allows for the moving, enlarging, rotating, coloring, and animating of data contained in other programs. Graphics programs are often used in draft and final preparation of summary charts and diagrams for management reports and briefings. Peripheral equipment such as a dot matrix printer and graphics tablet are frequently required.

Educational and Personal Development: This software transforms the microcomputer into an interactive educational tool for personal development. Logo is a well-known example of these generic programs; however, educational programs range from typing tutors, to language instructors, to microcomputer maintenance, to chess. This kind of software is likely to expand markedly in the coming years.

Personal Entertainment: Software that is primarily known for pure enjoyment or play value is often called "games" software. Many users have found game programs to be an excellent way to break down the

initial resistance when introducing computers in a developing country
setting. Playing a game as the first "hands on" experience with a
microcomputer eliminates some anxiety. Further, games programs can be
used to give microcomputer workers a break from routine data entry and
as part of training on the keyboard. Some of the more popular games
include computer versions of arcade games, sports activities, and
adventure episodes.

Adults, like children, eventually get tired of a game; thus, games
should be selected that offer a substantial challenge for a
considerable period of time. Another important factor is variety:
choose games that become more and more difficult as you progress or
those that include features that come into play at random. Many
microcomputer magazines contain periodic reviews of games and adventure
episodes. (Refer to Appendix D for a list of periodicals.)

Integrated Software: With an integrated software package you can
easily move between word processor, spreadsheet, database, and
sometimes even telecommunications, graphics, and programming languages.
Software packages produced by different manufacturers are not always
compatible: a word processing program and a spreadsheet program may
both work on your computer, but not on a common data set or in the same
document. If you are using a word processing program to write a report
and want to insert calculations from a spreadsheet into the report, an
integrated package allows you to do the computations, insert them into
the report, and then return to word processing. Without an integrated
package you must stop and insert another program to change functions,
then reinsert the word processing program to go back to writing your
report.

Some integrated software packages currently on the market include
Intuit, Framework, and Symphony. Some of these programs are stronger
in certain areas than others. For example, Intuit is designed for
large document writing and combines spreadsheet and file management,
while Framework is a strong spreadsheet program with a passable word
processor. Although your stand-alone software program may be more
powerful than one module of an integrated package, the integration of
three main functions into one easy-to-use unit may prove the best
combination in the long run.

MICROCOMPUTER USERS AND THEIR ENVIRONMENT

So far the major focus of this guide has been to examine management's
potential use of microcomputers. We have discussed their function,
their hardware, their software and how they operate. Now we will shift
our emphasis from the microcomputer to the user--in this case, the
development manager. In the next chapter we will examine the user's
needs to see whether they can be met cost-effectively by the
introduction of a properly configured and installed microcomputer
system. The evidence strongly suggests that microcomputers are only
useful to the extent that they appropriately meet some valued need of
the user.

One fundamental characteristic of a manager's job is its varied and frenzied nature. Managers perform a range of activities and roles in order to mobilize and direct scarce resources toward the timely accomplishment of development objectives. Work is typically conducted under considerable time pressure, conditions of uncertainty, and only partial control of resources. In the manager's job there is a mixture of the routine and the unexpected. On any given day, initial plans may need to be amended as problems arise, meetings drag on, or as is often the case, unannounced guests show up in the office expecting an audience. In this context, managers are concerned about adequately handling necessary tasks in the least time possible so that quality time can be given to high priority, substantive concerns and technical matters. There is usually one further very important consideration—— the manager's family and/or other non-professional interests. For development managers, it is typical to find that their professional and private lives heavily impinge on one another——often to the detriment of both.

This is the human work context within which microcomputer acquisition and use issues must be addressed. Is there some minimum set of needs of the manager and the management work setting that can be cost-effectively met by the introduction of a microcomputer system? How much time will it take to benefit from the availability of this system? How will formal and informal work and personal relationships be affected? These questions and many others need to be systematically addressed when considering the acquisition of a microcomputer.

CHAPTER III

Choosing a Microcomputer for Use in Managing Projects and Institutions

The decision to purchase a microcomputer system rests on your needs and the degree to which the system can be sustained. Understanding "your needs" means analyzing current and potential activities that you or your organization believe would be enhanced through the use of a micro-computer. The degree of system sustainability is a function of the operational environment and the probability that a given microcomputer would prove effective over the long term.

The needs and system sustainability issue is depicted in Figure 4. In this figure, we show the sequence over time and the importance of each factor in the short, intermediate, and long term. For example, if a needs assessment is favorable toward the acquisition of a micro-computer, you must provide for the factors listed in column 1 in order to have minimum system sustainability in the short term. The dirty power issue is something that you must address immediately. The need for documentation written in the local language is not of equal priority; however, for the intermediate stage, it must be considered. Thus, viewed as a process, the factors presented in Figure 4 determine the sustainability of the microcomputer as a valuable tool for use in development management.

The issue of long term system sustainability must be considered during planning. The first step in deciding whether to purchase a microcomputer is to clearly describe the tasks you believe a computer can help you perform. Once you have determined the tasks that a microcomputer can do for you, and have analyzed environmental conditions, then you are ready to choose software and compatible hardware.

SHOULD YOU HAVE A MICROCOMPUTER?

You would not go to work without a pen and a calculator. Is your work situation such that you would not dream of going to work without a computer? The best analogy for the acquisition of a microcomputer is the telephone. If telephone service is available, you do not consider whether or not you want it; the benefits of increased communication are obvious. The same may be true for a microcomputer, but only if it will enhance your particular situation.

<table>
<tr><td>

If

a management needs
assessment indicates
the use of microcomputers

And

you provide

o   stable and clean
    electrical power

o   dust, temperature and
    and other environ-
    mental protection

o   maintenance and
    spare parts

</td><td>

Then

the short term single
or project system is
operational.

If

you now address

o   training for all
    levels of users

o   proper documentation

o   recurrent cost factors

o   changes in roles and
    organizational power
    issues

</td></tr>
</table>

The figure above was based on the list of critical issues in institutionalization of microcomputers generated by the participants at the
Michigan Stage University Conference on Microcomputers, 1982. The list
that emerged was:

1.   Needs assessment
2.   Power considerations
3.   Environmental considerations
4.   Maintenance strategies and capabilities

Then

the intermediate stage of
basic institutionalization
of microcomputer system
is operational.

If

you now address:

o   customs restrictions

o   donor agency bureaucracy

o   host country importation
approval

o   integration with national
policy issues

THEN

A PERMANENT, VIABLE,
SELF—SUSTAINING SYSTEM
IS OPERATIONAL.

5.   Software documentation in local language
6.   Training considerations
7.   Transportation and communications
8.   Customs restrictions
9.   Donor agency bureaucracy
10.   Host country importation approval
11.   Local host country procedures, regulations, etc.
12.   Adherence to official policies/channels
13.   Computer development advisory committee

Three reasons to consider getting a microcomputer:

o   enhanced job performance;
o   learning opportunities; and
o   personal enjoyment.

The sustainability factors that must be considered along with these personal reasons are:

o   stability of electrical power;
o   environmental conditions;
o   local support networks;
o   maintenance and repair; and
o   organizational considerations.

Job Performance Enhancement

For the development manager there can be little doubt that a microcomputer will have a significant positive impact on project operations. Preparing, editing, and revising reports, entering and manipulating numbers, and creating and varying "what if" scenarios can all be done with greater speed, efficiency, and accuracy on a computer than by hand.   However, the problems and possible complications of using a microcomputer in a developing country may overshadow the benefits.

It is important to remember the spectrum of work tools--from pencil and paper to mainframe computers. The microcomputer incorporates functions found in calculators, adding machines and self-correcting typewriters. The question is, "Do you just need one of these pieces of equipment or do you require many of these functions and more?"

Personal Enjoyment and Learning Opportunities

Personal enjoyment includes family and home entertainment use. Given the low cost for a basic microcomputer system, you can easily acquire your own microcomputer. Games and family/home software packages are fun and useful, and the various programs for telephone and mailing lists, recipe files, and financial and home accounting can make the system more than a toy.

The use of the computer as a learning tool is the factor that most often influences people. The number of software programs that provide interactive learning between people and machines is expanding at all levels.   Tutorials including math, spelling, grammar, history, chemistry, and physics are available for both children and adults. Computer Assisted Instruction (CAI) offers individuals the opportunity to learn at their own pace with immediate feedback. The advantages of using a microcomputer are numerous, but you must consider its impact in terms of your work and your life.

<u>Personal Considerations</u>

The introduction of a microcomputer into your life is a major change. The perception others have of you will be altered. When you enter a meeting with completed drafts and a third iteration of the financial projections that have been reviewed under several "what if" situations, your co-workers will view you differently. They might be impressed. They might be jealous. There may be other aspects and limitations to the way in which the microcomputer will affect both your personal and professional lives.

<u>Dependence on the Machine</u>

General ease of use will create increasing levels of microcomputer dependency and thus increased probabilities for human-machine system breakdowns of major proportions. Compared to larger computers, microcomputers are extremely easy to operate and they do many things that we find very useful. However, there is more to using microcomputers than learning to work with a particular software package. Knowledge of proper utility programs and data back-up procedures is crucial. One major equipment failure or operator error resulting in the loss of the only diskette containing the entire year's records would be a painful way to realize the value of a minimum operating knowledge of the microcomputer.

The many opportunities to work more productively are exciting. Quite often you will find that you can continue to work at home--more than you do now, or even more than you want to. Often the computer can continue working while you are doing other things. When you return, it is ready with some results or new sets of files. If you do not set some rules and limits until the initial excitement wears off, you can become a slave to your machine rather than being liberated by it.

But more, or at least equally, important is the growing dependence you will have in the microcomputer. It will contain your records and reports on electronic files. You will turn to it for much of your analyses for budgets and other decisions. All of this is fine, as long as you recognize the potential for new frustrations. If the day of the inevitable power failure comes, and for some reason you are not using your back-up power supply, you will lose your internal memory, which of course will contain original data and/or analysis that will take hours, days or weeks to replicate. Despair will set in and you will seriously question the value of having a microcomputer. As mentioned earlier, the microcomputer cannot make you more organized: <u>you</u> are responsible for maintaining the system that allows the microcomputer to assist you.

The microcomputer has an unparalleled ability to satisfy diversified needs; it will likely become the workhorse of the organization. This will lead to bottlenecks during periods of equipment failure or frustrations when multiple rush jobs require its use. Such bottlenecks should be anticipated so that you can continue without the equipment

for as long as necessary. The possibility of having the right part
and/or service capability within hours or days is normally not possible
in developing countries.   It is important to anticipate such
emergencies, and plan alternative measures.

<u>Alteration of Relationships</u>

The introduction of the microcomputer into your work or home environment will influence existing relationships more than almost any other
acquisition, with the possible exception of the birth of a baby. Your
relationships in the office will change. You will not use your
clerical staff as you did in the past. In many cases you can do things
faster yourself. Your typist may either feel slighted because you
would rather use the microcomputer than his/her services or may view
this as an opportunity to take on other responsibilities. Your
associates will form into two new groups: users and non-users.

Your family will change if you have a microcomputer in the house. Your
children will probably become proficient in its use very early; your
spouse may see it as another way time is taken away from the family or
may try to monopolize its use. It is important to recognize that the
versatility of the microcomputer can lead to its being useful to each
member of the family; new relationships and needs will develop that
will suggest new rules and new patterns of interaction.

TASK AND ENVIRONMENTAL ASSESSMENT

It is necessary to consider the impact of a microcomputer on your life and work environment. You need to examine ways in which the environment can be made conducive to microcomputer operations. It may be more difficult to anticipate and avert these problems than it would be to hire eight more people to do the jobs you want the microcomputer to do. Thus, the following sections on task assessment and environmental assessment are important if you are considering acquiring a microcomputer. Indeed, if you have the money and the time, you can set up a microcomputer system almost anywhere, creating the appropriate physical environment. The manager of a development project must ask a series of important questions, the first being, "What are my job needs?"

Before conducting a needs assessment, refer to Table 4. Examine the advantages and disadvantages of microcomputers in general and the specific items considered.

ASSESSING YOUR JOB NEEDS

A needs assessment with positive results is the first step in the process of attaining system sustainability. In order to conduct your own assessment you should examine your job needs against several performance requirements. Examine those tasks that you (and/or your staff) do that are most labor intensive, time consuming, routine, and have a high probability of error.

We have provided a number of forms that take you through an assessment of your job needs. This assessment will help you determine if a microcomputer will be beneficial in your situation. Environmental considerations follow in a later section of this chapter. The first form, Assessment of Job Needs, asks you to look at your work priorities and to determine if microcomputer equipment will meet your requirements.

Pros	Item	Cons
Increased accessibility to substantial computational and analytic power. Extra-ordinary in speed of data and word processing; time saving "what-if" modeling; ease of access to informa-tion; flexibility in application.	**MICROCOMPUTER IN GENERAL**	Insufficient information con-trol; intrusion upon and erosion of indigenous culture; labor displacement; misuse of information; misuse of person-nel due to inappropriate or redundant use of micros; policy and procedural dif-ficulties in acquisition.
Reliable, durable, low-cost, compact, has multiple functions, including programming, running existing programs, providing entertainment; off-the-shelf availability minimizes lead time for installation.	**HARDWARE**	Needs non-fluctuating power supply; proper work environment difficult to achieve; hard to import,get spare parts, service, etc.; vulnerable to environment.
Low-cost, user-friendly; various software functions available for same hardware; storage of thousands of pages of information; easily accessible.	**SOFTWARE**	Information stored can be lost due to power problems, static, improper copying and documentation; hard to find in country; vulnerable to environment.
Inexpensive and easily accessible in the U.S. and Europe.	**SUPPLIES**	Almost impossible to find in country: ribbons, paper, storage, files, diskettes, programs.
With training and necessary equipment a user can do routine maintenance, trouble-shooting.	**MAINTENANCE**	Technicians may be unavail-able or, if available, dif-ficult to reach, unreliable, and unable to get spare parts.

Pros	Item	Cons
Others in area may have similar micros; parts; helpful advice and expertise.	USERS' GROUP	May be far away; projects may be politically at odds with each other and unwilling or unable to help.
Reduces report writing, accounting, planning, work time after system is operational. Power, speed, and accuracy make it possible to carry out routine functions rapidly so that staff time is released for other responsibilities. More accurate records can be maintained on both design and administrative tasks.	WORK LOAD	Creates need for additional filing, coding, inventory control; creates need for training at multiple management levels. Slows down other work while system is installed and people receive training.
Staff develops new skills and capabilities; training time can be minimal due to simplicity of the operating system, user-friendly software and interactive computer training programs.	TRAINING	Creates need for staff training in operation, maintenance; creates tensions as there are new procedures, changing assignments; new skills may not be recognized in civil service regulations.
Ability to develop compatible and integrated systems at different project locations linking field operations and central management.	DECENTRALIZATION	Dependency on computer information for decision-making.
Once system is installed, operational, and staff is trained, computational, planning and typing functions can be completed in a fraction of the time they took previously.	PRODUCTIVITY	Dependency on computer to do <u>all</u> functions can produce bottlenecks and slow work.

<u>Instructions for Assessment of Job Needs</u>

Complete the Assessment of Job Needs, page 1:

    1) List (under "Current") each task that you or your staff currently do daily, weekly or regularly that are labor intensive, routine, replete with error, time consuming.

    2) List (under "Desired") any activities or tasks you would like done, but that are currently not done due to lack of either time or expertise.

Complete the Assessment of Job Needs, page 2:

    3) Review the lists generated above and check the five items that are most important to you or your organization. Put them into a ranked list of priorities (1-5) on page 2. These tasks should have the greatest potential impact on your productivity or effectiveness.

    4) On page 2, using only your top five priorities, answer the following by checking the appropriate column.

        a.   Does the first ranked item justify:

           o more trained staff,
           o an adding machine,
           o a calculator,
           o a self-correcting typewriter,
           o a word processor,
           o a microcomputer.

        b.   Do the same for your second, third, fourth, and fifth priorities.

        c.   Look at your responses for the top <u>three</u> items on your list.

If your top three priorities require more than one piece of equipment to optimize efficiency, then you could use a microcomputer effectively. If each of the three priorities only requires a calculator, then that is what you need. If you believe that more staff could do a job you have specified, consider their availability and training requirements. Also consider the need for additional staff if you intend to purchase microcomputer equipment for your organization. And even if your job requirements justify acquiring a microcomputer, you still must assess the physical environment before you know exactly what you need beyond the microcomputer itself.

List of Current and Desired
Tasks/Activities

Current

1.

2.

3.

4.

5.

6.

7.

Desired

1.

2.

3.

4.

5.

6.

7.

(CHECK MOST IMPORTANT THREE PRIORITIES)

<u>TASKS CAN BE ACCOMPLISHED BY</u>

More Staff	Adding Machine	Calcu-lator	Self-Correcting Typewriter	Word Processor	Micro-computer
1.					
2.					
3.					
4.					
5.					

ASSESSING MICROCOMPUTER RELATED CONDITIONS IN DEVELOPING COUNTRIES

Environmental constraints and limitations must be included in the equation before you make the final decision to acquire a microcomputer for field use. As we said earlier, given unlimited funds almost any physical environment can be made hospitable to a computer. Further, as we have seen in the Assessment of Job Needs, many smaller and less delicate tools can be used to perform functions that under optimum circumstances could be assigned to a microcomputer. Thus, part of the assessment process must include an analysis of the environment and a careful analysis of the costs of improving it. The questions you must ask are:

o   Are there electrical power problems—"dirty power?"

o   Is the workspace/climate dusty, humid, hot?

o   Are there other users in the area and, if so, what kinds of systems do they have?

o   What is the situation regarding maintenance and repair? Are there available suppliers, distributors, technicians?   Is there a users' group to offer assistance?

o   Is there understanding within the organization of the implications of microcomputer technology?   Are staff members amenable?

o   Do you have the time to reorganize your management procedures to incorporate microcomputer use?

o   Do you have the time available for training yourself and staff?

o   Do you have the funds not only for the system itself but for back-up equipment and technical assistance?

Dirty Power

The most common problem for microcomputers in developing countries is electrical power instability—dirty power. For example, a typical microcomputer in Tanzania requires 220 volts AC, 40 cycle electricity. The voltage and frequency can vary roughly by 3% to 10%. But if you get a voltage spike of 1,000 volts, a significant frequency change, brown or black-out, you and/or your microcomputer will have serious problems.

The first step in understanding potential power problems is to talk with people in the area who use electricity for running equipment. You can also find out about power instability through a local network of microcomputer users—if there is one.

Dealing with dirty power is a common problem for anyone using microcomputers in development project situations. Some, but not all, solutions have been found. Whether these solutions are applicable to your situation is something only you can answer. The known solutions for power instability involve the use of something that "cleans up" the current before it reaches your equipment. (For a more detailed discussion, see the section on "Power Problems" in Chapter IV.)

Thus, if the area in which you will be using the microcomputer has unreliable power, you must include the cost of making it reliable. Although under certain circumstances the costs can exceed the price of the computer itself, these precautions must be viewed as essential if a computer is to function effectively in your development setting.

<u>Dust and Humidity</u>

Microcomputers are generally very rugged machines, but they must be provided with a clean and cool environment. In tropical climates, air conditioning (or at least a fan) is essential. Dust can cause real havoc. Covers must be used on all equipment. Again, depending on your location, the cost of keeping the system cool and clean can be high.

<u>Maintenance and Repair</u>

Microcomputer parts and maintenance service generally do not exist in developing countries. Most often you service your equipment yourself, give it to a friend who "knows something about computers," or you send it back to the United States or Europe (an expensive, time consuming, and not very desirable choice). Import restrictions and hard currency issues compound the problem of obtaining parts. The questions you must ask are: What is the quality and availability of local repair and maintenance? For what systems are services available? How much do I know about maintenance/repair and what do I have to learn?

The quality of available local repair and maintenance will affect your decision as to which model to buy, and whether to buy a redundant system or a spare parts kit. It will further affect your decisions about learning to troubleshoot equipment problems and doing routine maintenance yourself. (See Chapter IV for a detailed discussion of maintenance.)

<u>Local User Network</u>

Finding out who has what kind of equipment in your area is vitally important in your choice of a microcomputer. A single system con-figuration is often used by the majority of users in a given area. Use of a common microcomputer system makes repairs and support much easier for everyone. If you do find a local network of users, consider very seriously getting the same system they have, unless your needs are very different. Many local support groups are formed by users of various kinds of microcomputers. The most important contribution of a users' network can be providing a forum for the sharing of experience. If hardware commonly used in your area has software that can meet your needs, seriously consider buying that system. You may find that it is more beneficial to seek compatibility with other users in your area even if you find that the available software is not your first choice. The local support benefits may far outweigh the losses.

Organizational Setting

If you are considering the purchase of a microcomputer for use in a host country ministry or institution, give some serious thought to how the institution can maintain and support the system when you leave. Involve host-country administrators (and users-to-be) in all phases of the decision-making process. The institution should understand and accept microcomputerization before you make a commitment. Administrators must understand the annual maintenance and training costs associated with even a small microcomputer; these funds must be allocated. Furthermore, the system must be part of the on-going operation. Its use should be part of the problem-solving and decision-making environment of the organization or it will become a meaningless acquisition.

No organization will accept new technology without a clear understanding of its capabilities. It is important to demonstrate how the microcomputer can be used to meet management needs within the organization. Arrange for demonstrations by other people using microcomputers in the area. If possible, try to use examples from within the organization in your demonstration. Get people who will be involved in making the decision, and other users-to-be, to actually use the system.

The Host Country Perspective

User-friendliness, in the context of the host-country, refers to several of the system sustainability factors in Figure 4. Since most development programs are aimed at long-term effectiveness and change, sustainability is vitally important. Determining factors are:

o   documentation in local language;

o   local support and experience;

o   training at appropriate levels;

o   training in software administration and back-up procedures;

o   the issue of human-machine relations, or ergonomics.

<u>Documentation in the Local Language</u>

Many popular software programs and their documentation are available in
Spanish, French and Arabic, with more languages becoming available all
the time. If you cannot find a package in the language of your choice,
both program and documentation should be translated into the local
language--preferably by persons with local expertise and experience.
But accomplishing the translation obviously will depend on whether the
local staff is motivated and the effort is supported both financially
and operationally. Translation should be done as soon as the staff and
management show the necessary support and motivation.

<u>Local Maintenance Support and Experience</u>

The long-term acceptance and sustainability of the system depend on
local support and maintenance capability. In addition to support
provided by the dealer, maintenance training should be established
in-house and encouraged by the users' group.

<u>Training</u>

Initially, training will require a great deal of computer time as the
system users will need time to learn, improve, and practice. You must
manage, schedule, and plan for training and practice, and possibly
bring in experts to train you and your staff in use and maintenance.
For a detailed approach to training, see Chapter IV.

<u>Ergonomics</u>

The issue of people working directly with computers opens up an area of
relationships heretofore not considered. Ergonomics is a word not found
in 15-year-old dictionaries. But with the advent of microcomputers, the
relationship between human and machine must be considered. We have
dealt with this topic in Chapter IV in our discussion of training and
introducing people to easier activities first. Another key to success
is involving people who are going to use and be affected by the
introduction of microcomputers in the process of deciding how and where
these computers are going to be used.

Managers often expect a much higher rate of productivity from workers
almost as soon the new systems are installed. But even though
microcomputers are capable of working with great speed, their new
operators are not, and productivity is closely related to human health
and stress levels. Most office equipment was not designed to
accommodate computers of any kind. Lighting, seating, work surface
height, temperature, and work habits are all designed for an older
technology. Some solutions to the questions of ergonomics include:

    o   buying polaroid screen covers to reduce screen glare;

    o   placing an incandescent light on each operator's desk
         to eliminate eye strain from fluorescent lighting;

o   using tables lower than the standard "typists desk" and
     adjustable chairs;

o   having operators sit as far from the screen as
     feasible; and

o   advocating frequent breaks away from the microcomputer.

USING THE MICROCOMPUTER DECISION CRITERIA SUMMARY SHEET

Now that we have addressed some of the personal, environmental, and
organizational factors in microcomputer acquisition, reconsider your
priority analysis on the Job Needs Assessment. If your analysis led
you to decide that a microcomputer would help you in your work, the
questions on the following Microcomputer Decision Criteria Summary
Sheet will further assist you in examining the physical environment,
organizational setting, and job needs as you continue to explore your
situation regarding microcomputer acquisition.

<h1 align="center">MICROCOMPUTER DECISION CRITERIA SUMMARY SHEET</h1>

Respond <u>yes</u> or <u>no</u> to the questions below.

<u>Response</u>
(Yes/No)

<u>Personal Factors</u>

1. On The Assessment of Job Needs you have identified
   three tasks you do currently or would like to do
   that justify a microcomputer.

2. You have some idea of the kinds of software that
   will perform these tasks.

3. You have some idea of some microcomputer hardware
   that will run the software.

4. You can purchase the hardware with minimal
   problems.

5. You see the microcomputer as a learning
   opportunity.

6. You can afford the learning time that is
   required to learn to use the system.

<u>Environmental Factors</u>

1. Clean power is available.

2. Dirty power is not a problem,
   or dirty power is a problem, but
   you can afford the ancillary equipment
   to clean it up.

3. You or someone locally has proven repair and
   maintenance expertise.

4. Your host environment is clean, or
   your host environment is dusty, hot, humid,
   but you can afford the ancillary equipment
   to make it cool and clean.

5. A local support network is available and
   accessible.

6. Your situation or organizational setting is--
   in your judgment--amenable to the use of a
   microcomputer.

<u>Consider these additional questions</u>.

1. How much time will it take to benefit from the availability of the system?   (Consider funding approval, purchase, ordering, delivery, installation, training.)

2. How will formal and informal work be affected by the system? (Whose roles will change, what information will be stored, what office procedures will become redundant, who will manage the different kinds of work that will go on the machine?)

3. How will your personal relationships be affected? (Supervisors, co-workers, support staff, family?)

Assessment

If you had any negative answers, review them and give the purchase some additional serious thinking. If your answers were positive, consider the purchase of a microcomputer for yourself, your project, or your institution.

The benefits of microcomputer use in a project environment can be inestimable--given the proper conditions. The cost is so low relative to alternative ways of doing the same work that the temptation exists to just get a microcomputer and move on. However, we advocate making a realistic assessment of the problems and solutions before purchasing the system.

SELECTING A SYSTEM

Once you have decided that you are going to acquire a microcomputer and
that your environment is conducive (or can be made conducive) to a
system, you must choose the system itself. Remember that your needs
determine the software, and the software determines the hardware.

Software Considerations

Unless you are already familiar with various software packages, trying
the software in your environment is the best way to find out if it
meets your needs. A problem exists, however, because most software is
sold with no exchange privileges. The second best solution is to use
it or see it used in an environment similar to yours. A third and much
less desirable alternative is to use it or see it run in any
environment.

In any of the above situations, try to see the software operate under
conditions that push it to the limits you believe are important to you.
For example, if you believe you need a database management software
package that requires at least 1,000 records to do frequent searches
using three and four variables, then test the package under similar
circumstances to assess its ability to perform. If it is relatively
slow or unable to perform in a manner you desire, reconsider the
software you need. Realizing that this is a time-consuming process,
ask the dealer to put you in touch with someone who is using the same
software package for similar applications. Successful (and un-
successful) users are generally very willing to share information.

Chapter II included some descriptions of word processing, database
management, and statistical packages for your consideration. Many
other descriptions and reviews are available. Take the time to
evaluate the options when you decide on your specific software needs.
Appendix C lists some manufacturers of microcomputers who will send you
information about the software available for use on their systems.
Appendix C also lists some manufacturers of the most commonly used
software. The publications listed in Appendices D and E contain many
software articles and reviews.

If you are going to buy a system, find the software package that does
the work you need done. Do not buy a dozen programs. Buy only the
basic set of programs that you need to do the jobs you have defined as
important to you or your organization. Also, get interactive software
so that you can share information between programs without having to
enter the data a second or third time. Remember, one of the advantages
of the microcomputer is that it can save time in the retrieval and
access of data.

<u>Hardware Considerations</u>

Hardware requirements are established by software program selection.
Each software program has minimum requirements that your hardware must
accommodate. For example, if you need a database management program,
and you choose dBase III, you must have hardware with 256 K of internal
memory, two 5 1/4 inch disk drives, a printer, and a monitor. Some
common parameters are:

o   all systems require a CPU, a keyboard, a monitor and
     one controller disk drive (into which the program is
     placed) as well as at least one secondary disk drive;

o   packaged applications software most used in development
     requires a minimum of 64 K of internal memory;

o   graphics packages require a dot matrix printer and/or a
     graphics tablet;

o   most packaged software comes in 5 1/4 inch diskettes;

o   if you are using word processing software to write
     reports for distribution, you should consider having
     both a dot matrix printer (for drafts) and a letter
     quality printer for final copy.

<u>Hardware Systems and Approximate Costs</u>

Now consider Tables 5 and 6. Table 5 provides some information on the
various hardware systems being used in development situations and Table
6 looks at approximate costs, both obvious and hidden.

Table 5

Microcomputer	Memory	Storage	Operating System
Apple			Apple DOS
a. II, II Plus	48K – 65K	1 5 1/4" floppy	
b. IIe	128K	2 5 1/4" floppies	
IBM			MSDOS
a. PC	256 – 640K	2 360K floppies	
b. XT	256 – 640K	1 360K floppy 1 hard drive	
c. AT	256 – 640K upgrade to 2.5 meg.	1 360K floppy 1 hi-density floppy 1 hard drive	
Compaq	256 –640K	2 360K floppies or hard drive	MSDOS
Laptops CP/M-based	32 – 128K non-volatile	128K memory 3 1/2" add-on drives	CP/M
IBM Compatible	256K – 512K	ROM storage	MSDOS
Kaypro			
a. II, IV, 2, 4	64K	2 floppies	CP/M
b. 10	64K	1 360K floppy 1 hard drive	CP/M
c. PC	128 – 768K	360K floppies or hard drive	MSDOS
Wang PC	256 – 768K	2 360K floppies	Wang/MSDOS

Development Project Use/History	Field Support	Field Durability
Easiest to use for simple applications. a. Extensive thru 1984. b. Currently dominant in field use.	Users' groups, dealers, spare parts, repair in all major countries.	Robust; high tolerance to power fluctuations. Work well in remote in sites.
Dominant system in field use. Standard USAID/ World Bank project machine. a. Common; usually upgraded to XT. b. Most common. c. Popular, but not common yet.	Users' groups, dealers, spare parts, repair in all major countries. c. Available through authorized and other channels, make sure local spare parts/ service good.	Some problems with 110V/60 cycle used in 220–240V/50 cycle countries. Fan runs slow, overheats in warm climates. a. Average b. Average c. No track record
Popular in stand-alone applications.	Dealerships generally available in major countries.	Above average; same 60 cycle problem as IBM.
Tandy 100/200 good for TDY; HP 110 prevalent because of MS DOS capability.	Generally non-existent in Third World countries; send to US/ Europe for repair.	High; work well in remote sites.
Standard workhorse. Excellent back-up/ support machines. a. Being replaced by Kaypro 10 and 16 bit micros. b. Workhorse c. Not common.	Users' groups still dominant in field. " " "	a. KII high, KIV average b. Average c. No track record
Often used in development organizations because of interface with larger systems.	Medium for micros. Field staff trained in minis and mainframes.	Average

<u>Costs of Systems</u>

Microcomputers provide great power in computation, arithmetic manipulation and text revision at low apparent cost. A $3,000 to $5,000 computer system with $2,000 worth of appropriate software is extra-ordinarily inexpensive in the context of programs and projects that involve millions of dollars. But these costs are just a small portion of the total cost: additional expenses will increase the costs of microcomputer integration substantially. (See Table 6 below for some approximate costs that might be incurred in a modest microcomputer effort.)

When the microcomputer is used for tasks that have large improvement impacts, the expenditures can be easily justified. When the micro-computer allows completion of valuable tasks that otherwise could not or would not be accomplished due to scarcity or expense of skilled workers, time requirements, or other factors, costs are easily justified. However, where the microcomputer will supplant workers who are in plentiful supply, and there is ample time to do the job manually, justification of the microcomputer should involve con-sideration of these factors.

Thunder & Associates, Inc. recently conducted a workshop on the use of microcomputers in community health and rural hospital settings. One of the products was "An Analysis of Cost Considerations" involved in introducing microcomputers in development. The chart that follows has been modified for general use and presents three options. Costs are shown for major categories of expenditures relative to introducing microcomputer technology into developing countries.

The figures are illustrative. Depending on the specific uses, level of use and staff training needs, the price will vary: however, the types of costs and amounts should suffice in most situations.

Costs are shown for equipment and other items under numbers 1 through 4. The types of technical assistance have been separated into three types under item 5, technical programming for specialized uses, training and working with staff during design and use of the application. Associated costs are shown for three different situations:

o   Introduction of a microcomputer for one major ap-
     plication requiring number crunching and/or time that
     is considered important to the organization;

o   similar situation, but requiring three microcomputers
     and increased technical assistance and training; and

o   introduction of four microcomputers, programming for
     two or three applications, additional training and
     technical assistance.

In general, the cost of introducing a microcomputer including equipment, printer, power protection, and the necessary personnel support would run around $26,000. Add the need for your own staff training and additional burden during the introduction phase. There are several "recurrent costs" that should be considered: equipment insurance (10%), paper, ribbons and similar disposable materials (5%) and continuing application programming based on desired changes and growth (5%). In addition, there are "hidden" costs in staff training and time lost to applying the new technology. This represents the first step or phase, and your use of microcomputers will likely expand with time and use.

Table 6   An Analysis of Cost Considerations for Hardware, Software and Technical Assistance

Cost Category	Price of Single System	% of Total	Price of Three Systems	% of Total	Price of Four Systems	% of Total
1. Equipment (1)						
a. Micro-						
computers (2)	3750	0.17	11250	0.29	15000	0.23
b. Printer, etc.	1500	0.07	4500	0.12	6000	0.09
2. Furniture	950	0.04	2850	0.07	3800	0.06
3. Power Protection	750	0.03	2250	0.06	3000	0.05
4. Software	1500	0.07	2000	0.05	2500	0.04
5. Technical Assistance (3)						
a. Programming	3000	0.14	3500	0.09	15000	0.23
b. Training	2500	0.11	3000	0.08	5000	0.08
c. Staff T.A./ follow-up	3000	0.14	4000	0.10	8500	0.13
d. Manual System Redesign	5000	0.23	5000	0.13	6000	0.09
6. TOTAL	21950	1.00	38350	1.00	64800	1.00

COMPARISON OF TECHNICAL AND
HARDWARE COST COMPONENTS:

Technical Assistance (% of total):	0.62	0.40	0.53
Hardware/Software (% of total):	0.38	0.60	0.47

Notes:
1. Assumes no duties or taxes
2. Average price for 256 K RAM, 10 megabyte hard disk storage
3. Typical breakdown of technical assistance (TA) provided.

<u>Instructions for the Preliminary System Description Sheet</u>

Once you have studied your needs and made a preliminary assessment of
your software requirements, software selection comes next. Review your
management needs, software choices, and choose hardware to fit the
software. Before doing so, investigate the power problems and
microcomputer systems used, distributed, and/or serviced in your area.
Completing the Preliminary System Description Sheet will help you make
tentative software and hardware selections based on your management
needs.

The Preliminary System Description Sheet has four columns: Management
Needs, Possible Applications Software, Hardware Requirements, and Costs
of Hardware Components. It also includes space to list hidden costs.
Before considering hardware selection, refer back to the Assessment of
Job Needs--the list of current and desired tasks and activities you
would like to have the microcomputer help you do.

1.   In the first column list those tasks for which you need a microcomputer.

2.   Compare your list with the list of applications contained in
Chapter II, Table 3. Are any of your current or desired tasks (ranked
in the top five) contained in Table 3? Some similar tasks should
appear. Table 3 can help give you an idea of the kinds of applications
software you need. Use Table 1 in Chapter I for additional assistance
on specific management tasks related to generic management functions.

3.   Using Tables 3 and 1 as references, make some preliminary software
choices based on your management needs. List them in column 2.

4. Using Table 5 and the information you have found out about users in
your area, make some preliminary hardware choices and list them in
column 3.

5.   In column 4, note possible hardware costs; at the bottom of the
page note other costs. (Use Tables 5 and 6 as references.)

<h3 align="center">PRELIMINARY SYSTEM DESCRIPTION SHEET</h3>

Management Needs	Possible Applications Software	Hardware Requirements	Cost of Hardware Components

Hidden Costs:

Power Protection

Air Conditioning

Building Arrangement

Spare Parts

Supplies

Technical Assistance

Training Time

Maintenance

<u>A Final Critical Reminder--Microcomputers Currently Being Used In Your Area</u>

The system you choose should be compatible with the environmental factors in your area. For example, let us assume that both an IBM and an Apple IIe will run the software you need. Your preliminary survey has disclosed the Apple IIe is the system currently in use by fifteen other users, and there is a maintenance and repair capability for Apple, but not for the IBM. Clearly, you should lean towards acquiring an Apple IIe. The systems used in your area should be considered as important as any other single criterion in your decision making.

CHAPTER IV

Installing, Using, and Maintaining Microcomputers in Development Project and Institutional Settings

Once you have decided to acquire a microcomputer system, you must implement the decision by:

o   purchasing the system;
o   installing and learning to use the system;
o   using the system; and
o   maintaining the system.

Installing and maintaining a stereo, learning to drive an automobile, and using a telephone all have certain characteristics analogous to installing, using, and maintaining a microcomputer system.

Installing a microcomputer can be compared to installing a typical stereo system. You have probably set one up yourself in a matter of minutes. You made interconnections between different system components by attaching connecting cables and wires according to the instructions supplied with your equipment. Then, by turning the system on, putting on a record or a tape--you had music. The same is true for a microcomputer. Once the components are connected properly, the power supply is constant, the equipment is turned on, and the program diskette is inserted, you are ready to begin to use your system.

The automobile provides a good analogy for learning to use the microcomputer. Once you learn some basic, operational procedures and do some practice driving, the automobile is fairly easy to use. This is true of a microcomputer as well: learning to use it has tremendous returns--as long as you signal before turning, stop at stop signs, and watch the road.

The telephone is most similar to the microcomputer in terms of user potential. As with the microcomputer, the original idea of how the telephone would or could be used falls far short of its capability. With a telephone you can talk to friends, negotiate business, order consumer goods, and link up between computers--a far cry from the original vision of the phone as a useful but non-essential tool. And you are able to do all of this internationally at any time without external control by any other group or person.

Maintaining the microcomputer is similar to maintaining a stereo. The stereo generally needs little maintenance; it tends to be very reliable. However, when you do have a problem, you try some basic,

simple corrective actions that often work. You check the power,
speaker connections, etc. If you cannot get the system to work, you
call an expert.

These three examples are similar to microcomputers in one way: each
represents a very sophisticated technology that has been made simple
enough for use by the average person. However, in each of the
comparisons made above, the key difference between the microcomputer
and the other technology is that the microcomputer system always has
more. It has more connections to be made during installation; it
requires more learning to gain access to its tremendous potential; and
finally, in maintaining it, there are more actions you can take to
correct problems and there are many more problems requiring expert
assistance.

It is important to understand that you do not have to be technically
inclined to install, use and maintain a microcomputer system. The
hardware and software currently available are being accompanied by
better and better documentation. Having some knowledge about the
technology can help you avoid the frustrations that result from
problems--especially in a developing country where technicians are
scarce, if available at all. The more knowledgeable you are, the more
independent you can be about maintaining the equipment. The section in
this chapter on maintenance and repair goes into some detail about
minimum maintenance capability.

PURCHASING THE EQUIPMENT

Once you are ready to purchase hardware, we can assume that you have
determined what you need the microcomputer to do and have defined the
kind of software reeded. You know the software's hardware requirements
and so, keeping in mind what others in the area have, you purchase the
equipment.

Being a development manager, you probably will purchase your microcomputer in one of two ways:

   o   You will personally purchase the system while in the
       U.S.; or

   o   You will order a system to be sent to you or the
       project (mail order).

In the first case you should explore the options. You should talk with
different dealers. Have them show you how to install various systems
and how to use each with the software. You may instead opt to work
with a friend's system, or be connected to a microcomputer club or
users' group. In gathering information, your goal is to be familiar
with the system when you unpack it, and know how to install it by
yourself or with a friend.

If you decide to order a microcomputer system to be mailed to you, you may do so with or without technical assistance. If you have assistance with design and purchasing, the technical assistance should include a return visit to install the system. If you are on your own, then, under the best circumstances, you will have access to a friend or expert or the opportunity to talk to the local distributor. Under the worst circumstances, the system will arrive and you must connect it by relying on the installation documentation that comes with the system. If your system is not complicated, this should present few problems. But it is best to spend some time with someone who has a similar microcomputer system and learn to install and operate it--before it arrives.

WHAT TO ORDER

When you are ordering the microcomputer hardware, make sure to include the cables and connectors required to connect the various components. If possible, order the entire system from a single source so that the company can provide the correct interconnections. Local availability of connectors is usually limited except when there is a local dealer. Even then, the availability of specific connectors is uncertain.

When you order your hardware, order all the miscellaneous supplies needed to keep your system operational: printer ribbons, extra daisy-wheel heads, paper, extra diskettes, and labels. Order at least enough for one project year. This is most important when local availability is limited and supplies must be ordered from another country. Customs and ordinary delivery time can run between two months and a year--or more.

Include some "how to" software in your order. This can range from how to use the keyboard to tutorials on the software packages you are receiving. Make sure your software is configured to run with your particular computer and printer(s).

Also be sure to order basic and auxiliary documentation (manuals, handbooks) for all system components and software. This is most important if you are going to be installing the system on your own, and is necessary for troubleshooting system problems and maximizing component and software capability during system use. There are many good third party "how to" guides to specific software packages. Seldom does the manufacturer's documentation cover everything.

BEFORE INSTALLATION

Before installing your system, it is very important to ensure that it is protected from factors in the environment that can affect it. Many problems have been found in field use. Table 7 lists the four major problem areas are ranked by level or importance:

1.	Electrical Power	Highest
2.	Temperature	High
3.	Humidity	Middle
4.	Dust	Lowest

Power Problems

Power problems can be of a variety of types, chief among them:

- o   complete loss of power (black out)
- o   substantial reduction in available power
     (brown out--decrease in voltage)
- o   sudden voltage surge (spike--increase in voltage)
- o   variation in line frequency (fluctuation)

No power problem is without consequences, although some are worse than others. Any of the above occurrences can cause damage to your hardware, software, or the information contained in memory. The smallest power problem can result in the loss of all the information you have put in memory since you last "saved" it, or can damage the computer's internal mechanisms. The most insidious problems are the power spike and surge--the brief, split-second boost of voltage and the long sustained surge. In either case, the surge can be from approximately ten volts to over a thousand. If a surge occurs while you are working on the system, you can sustain innumerable forms of damage, both temporary and permanent.

What to do about power problems in development project situations depends on the problem itself. Something must be done, however. The known solutions for power problems include the use of equipment to "clean up" the current before it reaches your system. The most common solution is the use of an Uninterruptable Power Supply (UPS), a line conditioner that isolates your system from the power coming into your building and provides clean, steady voltage and amperage to your equipment.

Another solution is having a separate generator for microcomputer systems. A number of system users in Nepal and the Philippines isolate the equipment from the wall current by transforming the wall voltage through a large battery (see Appendix A).

A basic line surge or spike protection unit can be purchased for between $30 and $100. This is the most common solution sold by computer stores, but is generally inapplicable to the host-country situation and often solves the wrong problem. Some examples of solutions to power problems and the range of cost are shown in Table 8.

Table 8 Some Solutions to Power Problems and Their Costs

Solution	Cost ($)	Effective for: POWER			
		Outage	Reduction	Spike	Surge
1. Do nothing	0	------- Z E R O ---------			
2. Turn system off when you observe dimming and increased light bulb brightness	0	low	low	0	low
3. Install/use voltmeter to measure line voltage	10-50	0	med	0	low
4. Use transformer	10-100	0	low	0	0
5. Use basic battery protection system	200-300	----- med to high -----			
6. Use power protection with warnings and 1-5 minute back-up	500-700	med	high	high	high
7. Use uninterruptable power supply with 1-2 hour back-up	1,000-4,000	------- H I G H --------			

Table 8 is for general consideration. Discuss your particular concerns with persons familiar with the technology and the electrical situation in your environment. Match your needs to theirs for power protection and cost considerations.

<u>Dust, Humidity, and Heat</u>

Dust, humidity, and heat are easier problems to handle. Dust protection can be provided with covers for your equipment. Use lint-free or plastic materials. Further, if there is a lot of dust in the air, particularly if you are located next to a dirt road, keep the windows closed. It is also important to keep the room in which the system is located cool and dry. Use air conditioning or fans to lower the humidity and to circulate and cool the air. In some cases, it is necessary to have the fan blow directly on the equipment; the equipment should not get above ninety degrees while you are using it. As a rule of thumb, if the room is comfortable for you, it is comfortable for the system. Also, try to keep the room free of static electricity. Reducing the dust and humidity will help, but static free carpeting and/or a rubber mat under the equipment are better solutions to this problem. Thus, when you are sure that you:

   o   have protected the microcomputer from the environment
       by providing a non-fluctuating, appropriate power
       supply and a cool, dry, and static-free space;

   o   have the proper cables and connectors;

   o   have the necessary supplies;

   o   have the proper software; and

   o   have received the hardware

you are ready to install your system.

INSTALLATION

Installation instructions are generally well organized and fairly
simple, but they should be read thoroughly before any work is begun,
especially if you are installing the system without technical
assistance. Depending on your system, you generally have to connect
cables between the microcomputer, the printer, the disk drives, and,
possibly, the video monitor. Normally, the cables are visibly
different. If you have a UPS, plug it into the power supply, then plug
the UPS into the computer. Study the instructions and manuals enclosed
for your information, and you are ready to begin.

<u>Set up the whole system before plugging anything into the power supply</u>.
Be sure your power supply is functional. Plug in another piece of
equipment (e.g., a lamp) to the outlet you intend to use before
plugging in the system. Reread the documentation again and again as
you set the system up to make sure you are following the instructions.
If you need assistance, do not hesitate to seek it from a local expert
or colleague.

USING THE SYSTEM

Once you have made the connections and checked the power supply, the
next step is to turn on the system to see if it works. Turn on all
peripheral components (monitor and printer) <u>before</u> you turn on the
central processing unit itself. Turning the microcomputer on last
avoids power surges that might affect internal memory. Lights or an
image on the screen indicate that the monitor is on. The printer hums
when on. You can now see if the system is functioning by inserting a
diskette--an operating system diskette or one that is formatted to boot
up the system.

Because the IBM PC is one of the most common systems in the field we
will use it as an example here. Our hypothetical system includes two 5
1/4" double density disk drives, one printer, one monitor, and the CPU
with keyboard.

The first step is to turn the system on. Insert the operating system
diskette into the controller disk drive. Inserting a diskette into a
disk drive requires know-how. (This information is generally contained
in the very first part of the documentation that comes with your
microcomputer.) Hold the diskette by its label so that the label faces
up or is on top and can be seen. Never touch the actual diskette that
can be seen through any of the cut-out areas of the plastic cover. On
an IBM PC, and on most computers other than the Apple, the computer
should be turned on before inserting disks into the disk drives and
diskettes should be removed from the drives before turning the
microcomputer off (again to avoid power surges). Hold the disk so that
the label is up and, after opening the drive, place it in the disk
drive until the diskette will not go in any further. Do this in a
manner that will not bend it or damage it in any way. Close the disk
drive door.

The microcomputer should "boot" (or start) itself. After entering the
date and time to set the internal clock, you will see a blank screen
with the symbol A> in the upper left corner. Your next step may be to
insert another diskette for a particular applications software package,
or your work may involve the operating system. Now that you have
inserted a program you are ready to do some computing. Depending on
the software program you inserted, you can proceed according to either
your documentation or the menu on your screen.

Another installation concern is interfacing or "configuring" various
software packages. Often the operating system software contains some
internal parameters that must be set to ensure that it works with the
printer you are using. This is generally accomplished by selecting the
"install" choice of your operating system software menu. Have your
printer manual handy. You can configure the microcomputer to the
printer by answering a series of questions contained in the operating
system software itself. However, given the variety of printer types on
the market, you should, if possible, have the company from whom you
purchased set the internal parameters to interface your software to
printer. If this is not possible, and you are having difficulty, ask a
local colleague or technician to assist you.

Learning to Use the System

To continue the car analogy, learning to drive requires a lot more
experience than just learning to steer. The microcomputer is much the
same. You can learn to turn the wheel very quickly, but it takes more
time to learn to drive efficiently and carefully. The microcomputer
has no driving test, so you are on your own. If you crash or damage

something, you will lose a report or damage a diskette. These and other "accidents" can happen very easily, but you can minimize them by learning to use the system properly without taking risks.

Once the system is operational, a microcomputer is rather easy to use. You can "boot" the system (get it going) by following instructions. However, before using your applications software, you should and must learn some of the basic capabilities of the system. These include how to:

    o   format diskettes (make blank diskettes compatible to your operating system);

    o   copy files and diskettes;

    o   determine which files are on a diskette;

    o   determine how much information a diskette can hold; and

    o   back up information.

The documentation that accompanies most systems will provide you with this information. Again, ask other users in the area to help you learn.

<u>Beginning to Use Software Packages</u>

When you are ready to begin to use software, whether you are on your own or working with others, carefully read the manuals that come with the packages--paying particular attention to the first few chapters. Work through the exercises the manufacturer has included to become familiar with the system. Books with "beginner" in the title can be helpful. Play games--games are an excellent way to learn some of the basic capabilities of the system. Use the tutorial software that comes with many packages and "how to" packages. These software packages are invaluable during the first stages of learning.

Most basic level software packages include a tutorial file or an example of how to use the software in an application. Most electronic spreadsheets include some samples of a budget sheet or a "break even." Some word processing programs have a tutorial on the use of the basic commands. Using these tutorial programs can provide you with basic understanding of the software package within one to two hours. If there is no tutorial program per se, look to see if there is an informational file on the disk called HELP or READ.ME. Using a software package well requires a few more hours; to fully exploit its potential and become proficient and fast takes time and practice.

When you do progress to using applications software, remember to limit yourself to one or two software packages at first. Learning one package well will give you familiarity with the mode and range of user-friendly, menu-driven software.

USING A MICROCOMPUTER SYSTEM IN MANAGING A DEVELOPMENT PROJECT

Introducing a microcomputer into the workplace or the home adds several new concerns: where to locate the system; protection and security of the system; training; communicating with other systems; and maintenance.

Location and Scheduling Use

If the system is to be used by more than one person for more than one purpose, different users should have easy access to it. Thus, the system should be placed in a neutral area. Of course, if it is only to be used by you or by the accounting section, then you would place it accordingly. Remember that the system can only operate so many hours a day. You may have to schedule the time for different persons to have access--bearing in mind your priorities and why you acquired the equipment in the first place.

Printing documents can tie up the system. On many systems, when the printer is in operation, the system cannot be used for any other tasks. The printer (depending on its speed) can take fifteen minutes to an hour to print a 30-page document. One solution is to require that printing be done in the slack periods or when the system is not scheduled for use by others. Requiring people to make appointments to use the system is also a good idea.

Training

Training should be provided for each level of user and at different stages within each level as skills develop. Management staff should receive different instruction and training than the operations staff-- different levels will use the system for different functions. Further, each level's degree of difficulty in using software programs should be recognized. Training should begin with the simplest software program that meets the immediate needs of each group. Once one program is mastered and if the group needs to learn more, then (and only then) should the group move on to a more sophisticated package.

The Phases of Training

Training host-country staff--even English speaking host-country staff--to use English software with English documentation is not necessarily an easy task. Training includes three phases:

    o   Pre-training preparation
    o   Training
    o   Implementation

<u>Pre-Training Preparation:</u> Before training begins, the software package
to be learned should be matched with the particular jobs of staff
members.   This stage also includes identifying a trainer whose
responsibility it is to:

o   ensure that the hardware system is functional;

o   review, annotate, and condense the documentation to
     eliminate extraneous, humorous, and incorrect
     instructions;

o   hold informative staff meeting(s) to describe the
     system, demonstrate the system, discuss staff
     organization and responsibilities regarding the
     computer, and plan for the upheaval that training and
     computerization will bring;

o   design computer input forms if necessary;

o   prepare a training design to meet organizational needs;

o   oversee the installation of a computer system
     management operation that includes:
       – staff computer use policy,
       – disk storage and system security,
       – the role of the computer manager,
       – retrieval systems,
       – scheduling access,
       – logging work,
       – maintenance and support;

o   Urge management to hire someone to assist with
     trainees' regular work. The knowledge of regular work
     piling up often causes stress and hampers staff
     motivation.

<u>Training</u>: To be effective, a training program for host-country staff
should have the following characteristics. It should:

o   be supported by management so that trainees do not feel
     pressured by getting behind in their regular work;

o   use twelve hours per person per program at the computer
     as a rule of thumb for training on a software package;

o   anticipate a maximum four hours per day at the machine;

o   use pairs of trainees at one time: one trainee works
     for about 1/2 hour while the other watches, helps,
     communicates in the host-country language. Then they
     trade places;

o   provide trainees with a checklist of skills/commands to
    be mastered, so that they can check them off as
    training progresses;

o   teach trainees how to care for the equipment;

o   teach trainees how to format and copy (back-up) and
    emphasize saving and copying often;

o   develop flipcharts of start-up steps, jargon, confusing
    commands, troubleshooting procedures, error messages
    and access commands by program, etc.;

o   ensure that trainees take notes in their own language;

o   ensure that trainees input something "necessary" into
    the computer during training;

o   have trainees proofread their input on the monitor to
    ensure that accurate information was typed in;

o   ensure that trainees learn how to get out of "traps,"
    tutorials often assume no errors are made;

o   teach trainees how to use resource materials--to "dig"
    for information using indexes and other pieces of
    documentation;

o   teach trainees how to interpret the data that is
    printed out and to check for accuracy; and

o   ensure that management staff members are introduced to
    all packages that staff members are using so that
    management knows what the software can do.

<u>Implementation</u>:   After training it is important to ensure that the
system is incorporated into the organization's on-going activities.
This can be accomplished by ensuring that:

o   a computer resource person is designated to schedule
    access, print out directories, back up the system, and
    ensure that an index of files by disk (or volume) is
    created and updated;

o   trainees continue to use the computer at least two
    hours a week;

o   each staff member knows his/her computer re-
    sponsibilities and the responsibilities of others; and

o   a computer management plan is developed to ensure
     access, back-up, paperflow and communication among
     offices about what has been done and needs to be done
     on the computer.

Software Administration and Back-Up

It is important that users be trained not only in the use of the
software, but also in the basics of software back-up and administration. Every software program and data disk should be copied
("backed-up") daily and another separate copy made weekly. This
ensures that if any problems are encountered, good data will be
available from the last back-up and only the newest records will have
to be re-entered. The benefit far outweighs the tedium of the
activity.

The Computer Management Plan

Any person working for an organization has a job description, location,
a supervisor, and an outline of duties and responsibilities. This is
true for a computer as well. This new staff member--the computer--can
be a valuable resource if managed properly. Once training is completed
and the role of the computer is clarified, a computer management plan
should be developed. Such a plan might include information on:

o   The role of the computer
     - Policy on use of equipment
     - Description of the hardware and software
     - Location of the system

o   Staff responsibilities regarding the computer
     - Position, name and responsibilities of each staff person

o   The role of the computer resource person
     - Plan and manage computer access using the schedule and
       the logging process
     - Distribute a monthly computer use schedule
     - Ensure daily back-up of disks or cartridges
     - Be responsible for other aspects of system security
     - Program diskettes or cartridges, when appropriate
     - Act as a resource on software use
     - Create and maintain an index system of files for
       storage and retrieval
     - Print out a directory of all files on disk
     - Arrange for equipment maintenance and repair
     - Inventory and order supplies
     - Troubleshoot problems and keep the system operational

o   The role of the staff
     - Schedule computer access with the computer resource person
     - Note what was done on the computer log, by date, name,
       and application

o   The Schedule
     - The computer resource person coordinates, produces and
       distributes a monthly computer use schedule
     - When there are questions of priority, someone
       should be directly responsible for schedule changes

o   The Computer Log
     The computer log should be kept next to the computer.
     After each computer use or problem, the person who used
     the computer should record on the log:
     - date, name;
     - what was done and how long it took;
     - hardware problems;
     - repairs, cost, and time spent.

o   The Index
     An index of all files on disk or cartridge should be
     kept either externally or internally and should
     include:
     - disk number;
     - file name;
     - one phrase description of contents.

<u>System Security</u>

System security is an important area of concern. When you set up your
office system, make sure you protect your information. The system
must be protected from theft, and the software and files must be
safeguarded from loss of information.

To protect the equipment, put it in its own room and lock the door when
it is not being used. Provide only a few keys, or make one person
responsible for controlling access to the system. Software security is
equally important. As information is entered, it should be "saved"
every few pages. Then, all original disks should be copied and the
originals physically stored in another building. The working copy
should be used as the operational disk.

The data files you create should be duplicated daily. One way is to
have three disks on which you store data files. Two disks are used on
alternate days; entitle one MWFS for Monday, Wednesday, Friday, and
Saturday; and the other one TTS for Tuesday, Thursday, and Sunday.
When you use a file, use the disk for that day. At the end of each
day, save or copy the data to a third disk entitled "back-up disk" for
that file. In this way you always have at least one copy not more than
a day old if for any reason the information is "lost". Finally, at the
end of each week, copy the file to an archival disk for weekly or
monthly storage and keep this disk in a separate building. These
security measures are extremely important. Keeping the disks away from
inappropriate eyes can best be handled through limiting access to the
use of the disks themselves. Some software packages have security
measures built in, but most do not.

The key to protecting your data files and disks can be summed up by emphasizing the need to <u>back up, back up, back up all your data</u>.

In addition, diskettes need to be protected from dust and damage. Remember to keep them in their jackets when not in use. Occasionally a diskette will become unreliable, either in terms of information access, error messages, or just simply not booting. Before diagnosing this as a hardware failure, copy the files to a clean formatted disk and see if the problems still exist. Disk reliability varies with the manu-facturer, and with where and how often it is used. A reasonable lifespan for a diskette is one year. If you have stored information on diskettes, and want/need to keep old files, recopy them after a year to make sure that the information remains intact.

<u>Other Systems</u>

As the microcomputer system becomes a part of the office, there is a tendency to find more and more uses for it. This can mean considering the purchase of additional microcomputers, other components, and/or networking with other systems. The need for change grows as you learn to work with information and it becomes evident that access to information can increase project efficiency and effectiveness. The likelihood of expanding the system should be anticipated well in advance of actually doing it. Field experience suggests that you, as a manager, should become competent with your stand-alone system before adding components or linkages. Moving from single to networked systems creates new concerns. In an interconnected system, new issues and problems come into play concerning security and access to data.

A stand-alone system can be connected to other computers in a Local Area Network. The most important factor is whether the hardware and software will be reliable in your setting. As with the stand-alone system, workers quickly become dependent on the expanded features under the LAN, but unless you have a comprehensive contingency plan, a failure of this system means putting a number of operators out of work.

The use of a modem to communicate with other systems is inexpensive in terms of hardware and software, but be prepared for a long learning curve. Each country has its own problems in terms of local tech-nicalities and the reliability of telephone lines and systems. An alternative is to subscribe to a telecommunications network that uses packet switching. Networks such as CARINET (see Appendix B) offer menu-driven access to international communications at a reasonable price and with fewer headaches.

MAINTAINING THE SYSTEM

The longevity of a microcomputer system can be ensured through many of the precautionary measures mentioned previously. The longer term can be dealt with through prudent initial planning. The key consideration here is redundancy. Given the usual situation encountered in the field, the practice of carrying your own "spare parts" is very important.

<u>System Redundancy</u>

Field experience suggests that the purchase of two systems is better than just ordering spare parts. This is true for several reasons. Having another entire system provides:

o   an extra system that can be used for training;

o   a second system that can be used to salvage parts if
     anything fails in the primary system;

o   a second system that can be used for troubleshooting
     by comparing the two systems' performance when you have a
     problem;

o   a savings in cost: the cost of buying the spare parts
     package often exceeds the cost of buying a second
     system.

The "second system" approach works until you have more than five systems. After that, the spare parts approach usually makes better economic sense.

<u>Maintenance and Repair</u>

Your maintenance kit should include those basic components that account for the majority of failures on your system and that require a minimum of technical knowledge to replace, possibly not using more than a screwdriver and pair of pliers. Keeping your system alive becomes more crucial as you increase your dependence on its role in your work. You should learn, at least, some of the basic little "tricks" of taking care of and troubleshooting your system. The following practices will help:

o   unplug your system or turn it off at the power supply
     instead of using the On/Off switch. The On/Off switch
     is mechanical and can fail easily; and

o   take care of some of the simpler problems yourself.

When a problem occurs, you should first:

o   apply the 80/20 principle: 80% of your problems come
     from 20% of your software and hardware. Look to
     "trouble makers" first--those components of your system
     that have given you problems before;

o   check the wall plug to make sure it is in correctly;

o   turn the power off and then back on to reboot (or
    restart) the system;

o   check for "blown" fuses;

o   push the "boards" down and unplug and re-plug all
    cables and connectors;

o   check the manual for information on the component that
    is not working; and

o   take a ten minute break and try again.

Taking care of problems will often involve putting your hands into the
computer. Remember to:

o   unplug the computer and components from the electrical
    power supply; (This is to protect you.)

o   ground yourself to the equipment by touching some metal
    part outside the computer before you touch any other
    internal part of the computer. (This is to protect the
    computer: the slight static charge you may carry is
    actually far greater than many of the internal
    components need to operate and you can actually cause
    them to fail.); and

o   take off all jewelry.

Do regular monthly maintenance:

o   open the machine--unplug it first and touch the power
    supply to discharge static electricity;

o   press down all boards and chips; and

o   clean disk drives with special cleaning products.

When technicians come to fix the equipment, watch, take notes, learn
what was wrong. Perhaps you can fix it the next time yourself. The
most important factor in maintaining your system is understanding it.
This requires experience. You are going to be introduced to microcomputer technology in many ways. Within a short time you will become
proficient in its use and care.

In some ways, these measures may sound simplistic, but more than one
problem has been solved and major catastrophes avoided by using common
sense solutions. Plan for maintenance from the beginning. After that,
the role of maintenance is based on proper use and understanding of
your applications and the environment. If you follow this advice, your
system will do more and last a long time. With minimum maintenance,
your system should function for the life of your project.

SOME ADVICE

<u>Technical Assistance</u>

The importance of a users' group cannot be overstressed. The widespread use of the microcomputer and its dynamic applicability have caused an unlimited number of problems and opportunities, minor and major, that need addressing. The sheer number, diversity, and specific application types have provided the impetus for the formation of microcomputer users' groups. Any one person cannot be expected to know how to troubleshoot the equipment, repair it, and take full advantage of all of its possible applications. Users realized that, collectively, they had the knowledge--and the users' group was born.

A users' group for development project personnel in a particular location is crucial. Because of the inaccessibility to service, advice, parts, and knowledge, it is in your best interest to connect with users in your area or to start a users' group yourself. Several options exist for development project personnel who use microcomputers. Form your own users' group. Arrange to communicate with any other users' groups in the city/country you are in. Finally, link internationally with users' groups using similar systems and software. USAID, the U.N., the World Bank, and other organizations have formed or are forming users' groups and clearinghouse services concerning microcomputers. These are invaluable sources of information and assistance.

In an AID project, you can get technical assistance or a contractor through an IQC to provide training and assistance to your program or project. You can contact Data Management or the Office of Science and Technology in Washington and request information and assistance. You can check in at the mission and present your situation to see what is recommended.

<u>Traveling With a Microcomputer</u>

Where developing countries and single-user microcomputer systems are involved, it is likely that there will be occasions when you wish to travel either domestically or internationally with a microcomputer. When considering travel, several questions are relevant. First, what components do you need to take with you on the trip? Second, how should you transport the equipment? Finally, what difficulties might you encounter along the way that can be anticipated and planned for? The following discussion draws on some of our recent travel experience and addresses each of these questions.

Deciding what microcomputer equipment to take with you on a trip is largely dependent on the uses you expect to make of the microcomputer. For example, if you expect to use it to keep notes and prepare and print trip reports, i.e., for word processing, then you will need the computer, disk drive, monitor, printer, diskettes, paper, printer and power cables. Of course, you will need your favorite word processing software package. If part of the trip is to introduce the micro-computer to potential users, we suggest taking several easy-to-use programs and some games software.

In considering transportation of the equipment, one must first inquire about the durability of the microcomputer and peripheral equipment. We hand-carry or carefully pack all fragile equipment. For the common brands, manufacturers have recommended travel cases. Or you may be able to use the original packing box--at least for two or three trips. We have shipped an Apple system back and forth to Portugal in the baggage compartment on several occasions and have had no problems. We carry a Kaypro 2, Compaq Plus, or a Tandy 100 with us on international and domestic flights. Carrying the portable machine on board has so far presented no problems, although it is somewhat heavy and cumbersome.

There are several circumstances that the unseasoned international traveler--especially one without a diplomatic passport--should keep in mind when traveling with a microcomputer. Microcomputers have different connotations in different countries. On a recent trip to Central America our microcomputer was unable to clear Customs for two days until there was an assurance on the part of our hosts that we would not be using it for non-developmental purposes. Thus, you should take along an official letter stating what equipment is being transported, serial numbers, and intended use. This can be helpful, not only for entering a foreign country, but also for returning to the United States. Such a letter also provides you with ready security information in case your equipment is missing or stolen. Finally, we have found that even though airport X-ray machines will not usually damage software diskettes, it is a good precaution to carry them in a separate, sturdy container. We have been pleasantly surprised with the ease of transporting our microcomputer equipment internationally and using it with little or no difficulty upon arrival. Smaller, more durable equipment is constantly being developed, and traveling with a microcomputer has become significantly easier than it was when this book was first published three years ago.

<u>Do's and Don'ts</u>

In Table 9 we present a number of hints and precautionary points that can help direct you away from some possible unforseen tragedies. The first one is, however, "let experience be your guide."

<u>Planning</u>

1. Determine what you need a microcomputer to do for you. Then choose the software before you choose the hardware.

2. When considering the hardware, find out what others in your area are using and seriously consider purchasing that kind of equipment.

3. Have a plan for cleaning up the power instability.

4. Have a plan for training.

<u>Purchasing</u>

1. Explore your options. Talk to different dealers and have them show you how to set up the system and how to use it with various software packages. Work with a friend or colleague.

2. Order all miscellaneous materials and supplies you need for one project year, especially extra documentation.

3. Purchase connector cables when you order the system.

4. When you first buy equipment, also buy the tools, spare parts, test equipment, and hardware manuals (with schematics).

5. Specify that you want software programs configured to your system and printer.

<u>Installation</u>

1. Spend time with someone who has a similar system and learn how to put it together.

2. If possible, get assistance from someone who knows how to install the system.

3. Set up the whole system before plugging it into the power supply. Plug another piece of equipment (e.g., a lamp) into the outlet you intend to use for the system.

<u>Power</u>

1. Provide electrical protection:

    o   based on local user experience or knowledge;
    o   in the light of budget needs.

2. Strongly consider the use of an Uninterruptable Power Supply (UPS) to provide a non-fluctuating source of power to the equipment.

3. Dedicate a single line to your equipment, one that is pre-conditioned.

4. Provide common "earth" ground between all system components.

5. Condition your power appropriately.

6. Power on/off switches can fail. Consider unplugging your system when you turn it off instead of using a switch.

Hardware

1. If possible, consider buying one extra system for use during system breakdown or for possible spare parts.

2. Consider buying a diagnostic testing board for trouble-shooting, such as the one built into the Apple II.

3. In a central unit with built-in monitor and keyboard, you lose some maintenance flexibility. If you have to send an item away for repair, it is often convenient to send only the sub-unit needing repair instead of the entire unit.

4. 64 or 256 K of memory is adequate for running the packaged software most used in development projects. For most systems, when and if you need more memory, you can buy RAM chips or another "board" that contains additional memory.

5. For the average development project, the size of the database can be fairly easily determined and the size of disk drives properly selected. Disk drive size is not a major variable in system selection--only if you are using a program that requires 8" disk drives, or if you have a very large database would you consider large disk drives or hard disks.

Software

1. If it is not built into the system, buy a diagnostic software package to test your system problems.

2. Buy interactive software packages.

3. Buy "how to" packages and use them as well as tutorials to learn how to use particular kinds of software.

4. Buy only the software packages you need.

5. Learn one or two software packages at a time.

6. If your work involves a substantial amount of writing, give
    serious thought to getting a word processing program.

7. Games programs are good for training and for breaking down some
    of the initial resistance frequently encountered in development
    project situations.

8. Make sure the software is configured to your computer and printer.

<u>Diskettes</u>

1. Keep diskettes in their jackets.

2. Have extra blank, formatted diskettes available.

3. Make back-up copies of all diskettes--update and recopy as
    necessary.

4. Keep a card catalog of files that appear on each diskette, or
    some other form of external retrieval system (e.g., print-outs
    of disk directories that are dated and kept in file folders).

5. Use only felt tip pen to write on diskette labels--pressure on
    diskettes from ball point pen may damage them.

6. Keep your diskettes and records with you if you share the
    equipment with others.

7. Keep archive copies of diskettes in another location for
    safeguarding.

8. Recopy diskettes over a year old.

<u>Maintenance</u>

1. Whenever the system is opened for modification or routine
    maintenance, it should be turned off at the main switch.

2. Take off all jewelry and touch metal before going inside the
    "turned off" system.

3. Do regular monthly maintenance.

4. When someone else is doing maintenance, watch and take notes.

5. Inform yourself about computer maintenance by reading articles,
    equipment manuals, etc., and learn to diagnose problems.

6. Keep a maintenance notebook.

7. Know the different tolerance levels (concerning power and frequency requirements) for each piece of hardware, e.g.:

   o   electrical power 220, plus or minus 5% to remain operational.

   o   50 CPS (frequency), plus or minus 5% to remain operational.

8. The microcomputer industry is rapidly establishing sales and service facilities in developing countries which will eliminate the need for individuals and projects to provide their own maintenance capability.

Environment

1. Do not eat, drink or smoke near equipment.

2. Cover equipment with a lint-free cloth when not in use to protect it from food, drink, tobacco smoke or any foreign matter.

3. Keep equipment cool.

4. If the equipment is in an air conditioned room, seal all windows shut, have a back-up air conditioner available, have a spring on the door to keep it closed, use a wet bulb humidity measure and, if necessary, a dehumidifier in the room or inside the computer itself.

5. Keep the computer away from the air conditioner.

6. Provide an environment without static electricity--rubber mats under the machine, static free carpeting.

7. Provide adequate ventilation, e.g., fan blowing on computer or in room.

Supplies

1. Stock all fuses (of proper amperage) for all equipment.

2. Stock all needed supplies including diskettes, ribbons, cables, print heads, paper, transformers, etc., for a minimum of one year to the maximum life of the project.

3. Stock chips and boards as part of your spares kit.

CHAPTER V
Representative Microcomputer Applications in Development Projects and Institutions

The wide range of current applications and the potential of micro-computers for improving human productivity and organizational performance will be explored in this chapter. The descriptive accounts are intended to provide the reader with examples of actual developing country experience in microcomputer system design, acquisition, and use.

The case studies document a broad range of development applications around the world. The authors of each of the cases were asked to follow a similar format including a conclusion/synthesis section: "lessons learned." In the final portion of this chapter, we will present a general discussion of the lessons as they apply to the range of institutional and project-level applications.

How microcomputers are acquired and used for management purposes in development project contexts varies considerably. The following review of several specific microcomputer applications gives the potential microcomputer user an overview of the various issues, dilemmas, and strategies that have been used in acquiring and using microcomputers within project contexts.

APPLICATION #1: <u>BUREAUCRATIC REFORM EFFORTS AND MICROCOMPUTER USE IN INDONESIA'S MINISTRY OF FINANCE</u> (1)

INTRODUCTION

The Ministry of Finance (MOF), Indonesia, adopted microcomputers as part of a larger effort to reform the Ministry's revenue collection processes. In this paper I will briefly explore MOF's experience, with a focus on the Tax Directorate, where microcomputers have been introduced most widely. The goals of MOF headquarters, the conditions that support or obstruct achieving them, and some wider lessons that can be derived from MOF's experience will be presented.(2)

INTRODUCTION OF MICROCOMPUTERS IN MOF

For Indonesia, as for other developing countries, the early 1980's introduced an era of tightening economic constraints even as demands on government were growing. Senior members of government ministries became committed to improving their ministries' efficiency and effectiveness.

An important area of concern in MOF involved on-going problems in the Tax and Customs Directorates. As the economy had grown, it had become increasingly difficult to keep track of taxpayers, to monitor customs receipts, to control tax and customs collection, and to prevent irregularities in the payment and collection of taxes and customs fees.

The head of MOF's Center for Financial Analysis (<u>Pusat Analisa Informasi Keuangan</u>, PAIK) made a strong case to the Minister of Finance that better control over these revenue-generating areas was essential. He proposed that an important component of establishing such a system would be introducing microcomputers into the district offices of the Tax and Customs Directorates. In response to PAIK's proposal, the Ministry of Finance purchased 200 IBM Personal Computers in the summer of 1984.

Heads of some district tax offices and local customs offices were not enthusiastic about the decision to place microcomputers in their offices. District tax officers voiced reluctance to learning to operate a computer and concern about breaches in the security of tax

---

(1)   Dr. Janice Brodman has been involved extensively in improving microcomputer use in the private and public sectors of developing and industrialized countries. She is currently a Visiting Scholar at Harvard Institute for International Development, Harvard University.

(2)   For a more thorough analysis of microcomputer adoption in MOF, see Brodman, J. (1985). <u>Microcomputer Adoption in Developing Countries: Old Management Styles and New Information Systems</u>. Report prepared for The International Development Management Center, University of Maryland, College Park, Maryland.

information. In some cases, it was clear that local officers were antagonistic to the introduction of a process that was likely to severely limit opportunities to use their official positions for personal gain. Similar resistance was encountered from local customs offices.

USE OF MICROCOMPUTERS IN THE TAX DIRECTORATE

Despite the reservations voiced by many district tax office heads, PAIK introduced microcomputers into all sixty-nine local offices by the end of 1984. One objective of introducing microcomputers was to improve the accuracy of taxpayer files while integrating the microcomputers into the larger computer system at the central and regional offices. The micro-computers were also part of a new reporting and collection system at the district level. PAIK, working with expatriate advisors, designed the system to improve income tax compliance and standardize tax collection procedures at the district level.

Under the old system, tax collectors went into the field to assess and collect taxes. Taxpayers were audited at the district level, and the local tax office reconciled taxes due and taxes paid. Only aggregate statistics were sent to the regional level along with the taxes that had been collected.

Under the new system, there is no initial contract between local tax collectors and taxpayers. The taxpayer sends his/her tax return and payment to the local office. A district officer immediately enters the information from the tax return into the microcomputer. The data are then entered a second time by another operator and the two records are automatically checked for consistency by the microcomputer.

Each week, the districts make a streaming tape of the taxpayer information collected during the week. They send the tape by mail to the regional office where the information is entered into a minicomputer cumulative file. Auditing of returns is conducted at the regional level.

The new system improves the accuracy of information submitted from the districts. All problems, however, have not yet been resolved. One of the most important problems involves the transmission of information between district and regional offices. Mailing exposes information tapes to damage and to breaches in confidentiality. As yet, however, no better method appears to be available.

The introduction of large numbers of microcomputers also makes it difficult to preserve security of the data at the district level. There is a danger that "electronic corruption" might occur once the local offices understand how to use the machines. To prevent such irregularities, much attention has been given to establishing verification procedures within the system. Headquarters is making district offices well aware of the many cross-checks that are performed

on the tax information at the regional and central offices, including
auditing routines and trend analysis. Other preventive measures
include processes to ensure prompt submission of individual tax return
information by the district office, and regular review of district
office records.

<u>Microcomputer Training in the Tax Directorate</u>

PAIK systems analysts and programmers, along with staff from IBM (from
whom the microcomputers were purchased), are "training the trainers"
from each district tax office. The approach to training is based on
the assumption that most people are resistant to using computers.
Therefore, the computers are introduced with easy first steps,
including playing computer games. As people become more comfortable
with the microcomputers, they use them for tasks related to their work.
Because skilled staff are limited, particularly in local offices, PAIK
headquarters have designed simple, interactive menu-driven software
packages in Indonesian to be use at the district level.

The district offices' shift to the computerized system is being done in
stages. In the first stage, during which PAIK expects the operators to
make many mistakes, the manual system will continue to be used. In
later stages, as the operators become more accurate, the system will
gradually become fully computerized. By moving slowly, stage by stage,
PAIK officers expect that resistance will decline and skills will rise.

One of the most difficult training problems involves developing the
skills at headquarters necessary to design useful information systems.
Those skills require integration of technical "computer" knowledge with
substantive knowledge about the tax system. To resolve this problem,
PAIK is using teams of tax officers and PAIK technical staff to design
the directorate's information system.

IMPACT OF MICROCOMPUTER USE

Although it is too early to evaluate the new system, it is worth noting
that the expatriate advisors, as well as PAIK, consider prospects for
success to be good. The design of the information system is the key to
that success. Yet the microcomputers themselves make several contributions. They substantially reduce errors associated with handwritten
or typed entries. The advisors and PAIK also expect that the
psychological impact of the microcomputers will reinforce the formal
aspects of the system to prevent corruption at the local level.

Initial experience with the system suggests that PAIK's expectation
that the microcomputers will pay for themselves by improving tax
collection at the local level is not unrealistic. In many districts,
tax revenues have increased since the computer system has been
installed; in some districts revenues have doubled.

The response from local tax offices affected by the microcomputer
system has, however, been mixed. Some office directors have been quite

positive, and are interested in using the machines for office administration. More often the response has been negative. Several district offices have complained about mistakes in microcomputer tax records, and there is general disgruntlement with having the machines placed in their offices.

Some of these complaints can be attributed to local officers' loss of decision-making power to headquarters, which they perceive to be often out of touch with local conditions. In some cases, there is resistance due to lost opportunities for private gain. Some of the reaction is related to impatience with the inevitable problems associated with getting a computer system up and running. PAIK believes that those concerns will decline as the system improves and people become more comfortable with it.

LESSONS FROM THE MOF INDONESIA EXPERIENCE

The relatively short time during which MOF has used microcomputers precludes drawing definitive conclusions about the impact of microcomputer use. Nonetheless, MOF's experience suggests important factors associated with successful microcomputer adoption. The preliminary conclusions presented below will hopefully provide guidance for future adoption efforts and guideposts for further studies of microcomputer use in less developed countries.

1) Clear, strong support of organizational leadership is a key contributing factor to gaining rapid, widespread acceptance of microcomputer introduction.

MOF leadership initiated microcomputer introduction and gave it early, strong, consistent support. The resistance to the microcomputer system from district level offices made that leadership role particularly critical. Without explicit leadership support, the introduction of microcomputers into district offices would have been far more problematic.

2) It is important to ensure the availability of sufficient resources early in the introduction phase.

The question "how much is enough?" is a complicated one. Certainly, there must be enough microcomputers to carry out the tasks for which they were introduced as well as to make machines available for training Ministry staff. Yet, introducing too many microcomputers can produce serious problems. The large number of machines adopted by MOF created several difficulties. The training effort was extremely demanding for the skilled PAIK staff. Although training has been conducted very successfully, PAIK staff were often over-extended. The need to monitor use of the microcomputers at the district level will continue to stretch PAIK's staff resources very thin.

Some collateral resources do not seem adequate to support the large
microcomputer system. For example, the existing communications
infrastructure cannot effectively provide reliable means for
transmitting tax information between the district sites and the
regional offices. It should be noted, however, that hand-written
reports are equally susceptible to the vagaries of the postal system.
It is likely that this issue will become increasingly prominent, and
more dependable information conduits will have to be developed.

Thus, planning for sufficient resources requires careful examination of
all the factors that must contribute to a successful system. Those
factors include components of the system, including hardware, software,
and appropriately skilled labor. They also include relevant supporting
structures such as telecommunications. In most lesser developed
countries (LDCs), telecommunications is likely to be a very weak link
in any network system.

3) Microcomputers can be used effectively by operators with limited
formal education.

One way microcomputers have revolutionized computer use has been the
ease with which they can be used by people who have no technical
skills. A plethora of software packages that are increasingly easy to
use and the ability of skilled programmers to develop menu-driven
programs makes microcomputers potentially accessible to broad
populations of users in developing countries.

MOF has demonstrated that rural staff can successfully operate
menu-driven software. Of major importance to successfully training
district staff are PAIK's efforts to: a) begin slowly, with
anxiety-reducing applications such as computer games; b) link training
closely to trainees' jobs; c) devise menu-driven software that can be
easily followed by district office operators.

4) A major difficulty in developing an effective microcomputer system
is the existence of communications barriers between technical
"computer" and professional "content" staff.

Establishing effective communications links between technical
"computer" and professional "content" personnel is both difficult and
essential to developing an effective microcomputer information system.
To overcome these difficulties in the Tax Directorate, MOF uses teams
of technical computer staff and tax officers to develop computer
information systems. Teams of this kind have also been used to develop
information systems for the mainframe computer system and for each of
the other Directorates. Members of the teams from the two groups have
improved their understanding of one another's areas of expertise,
perspectives, and needs.

Yet MOF's experience also demonstrates the difficulties associated with
establishing that kind of cooperation. One problem is the tax
officers' lack of knowledge about the principles of microcomputer

operation. The tax officers tend to defer to the PAIK staff. PAIK staff often feel that the design of the information system should be left to them. As a result, the information system sometimes does not meet the needs of the tax officers who will be using it. To the extent that they are involved, the tax staff often want to simply transfer all the information that is now on paper to the microcomputers in a way that does not exploit the advantages of the microcomputers. Resolution of these problems appears to lie, at least in part, in ongoing interaction and communication among team members.

5) Microcomputers can help improve information accuracy and, within a well-designed system, support processes that induce greater compliance with formal regulations.

The improvements in accuracy, compliance, and regularization of tax collection in the district offices are associated in part with the characteristics of microcomputers. The machines can perform simple routines that automatically check the accuracy of entries. There is also a psychological effect on officers who believe that the machines can detect falsification.

Of even greater importance, however, is the larger system of which microcomputers are one part. MOF headquarters has designed a system to reduce opportunities for irregularities in tax collection. The result is that microcomputers are more likely to contribute to better compliance rather than "electronic corruption." MOF's use of microcomputers illuminates the importance of system design in determining the impact of the microcomputers.

6) In order for microcomputer use to be institutionalized, those who support microcomputer use must have control over critical resources.

MOF's experience makes it clear that microcomputers are not an apolitical tool. Ministry headquarters perceives microcomputer use to be positive; many district office heads perceive it to be negative. Institutionalization of the microcomputer system will depend on the extent to which headquarters controls key resources, including staff and budget allocations. MOF's experience suggests that those involved in institutionalizing microcomputers must gain the support of those who control critical resources.(3)

CONCLUSIONS

MOF's experience with microcomputer adoption demonstrates the rapidity with which microcomputer use can improve the accuracy of information files at the local level. It also suggests that central authorities can use microcomputers to help establish system reforms that are

____

(3) For a discussion of the importance of this type of control over resources in Kenya, see Chapters II, III, and IV in Brodman, op. cit.

unpopular with local offices. Successful reforms rely heavily on the
quality of the system design and the power of key individuals
introducing change.

If microcomputers are to help reform bureaucratic processes, the
information system of which they are part must be designed to prevent
misuse. In most LDC governments, designing such a system will require
access to skilled external assistance. In addition, people who want
change must have sufficient control over essential resources to impose
change in the face of resistance. Thus, while microcomputers have the
potential to support reform, their impact will depend largely on the
systems and structures into which they are introduced.

APPLICATION #2:   THE EASTERN CARIBBEAN FARMING SYSTEMS RESEARCH AND
DEVELOPMENT (FSR/D) PROJECT (1)

In 1983, the Caribbean Agricultural Research and Development Institute
(CARDI) initiated a Farming Systems Research and Development (FSR/D)
Project in eight island nations of the Eastern Caribbean. The
five-year FSR/D effort is funded through CARDI core funds and support
from the United States Agency for International Development (USAID).
The project budget is approximately 10 million dollars.

The FSR/D Project was designed to improve the economic and social
well-being of small and medium sized farms through the establishment of
an effective and sustainable farming systems research and development
program that responds to the agricultural needs of the English-speaking
Eastern Caribbean. The project's expected outputs were: (1) alternative crop, livestock, and crop/livestock technologies, (2) a
methodology to generate and disseminate these technologies, and (3)
strengthening the institutional capability of CARDI to support a FSR/D
program and successfully implement the project.

MICROCOMPUTER NEEDS ANALYSIS AND NETWORK DESIGN PROCEDURE

The CARDI microcomputer network was designed in four stages:

1) Review of past assessments done by outside consultants;

2) Analysis of CARDI's information and data management needs and its
current capabilities;

3) Design of a microcomputer network (including hardware, software,
and people/organizational components); and

---

(1) Prepared by Marcus Ingle, University of Maryland, and Robert Hart,
Winrock International.

4) Development of a plan to install the network incrementally in such a way that staff can be trained at the same time as hardware and software are installed. In this case study we define "network" as two or more geographically displaced microcomputers linked via telecommunications or using a common format for data entry.

The analysis of CARDI's information and data management needs and its capabilities was done as part of the design of the FSR/D project being implemented in the Eastern Caribbean. As a research institute, CARDI emphasizes the generation and transfer of agricultural technology. Both the technical research results and the actual uses of the resources must be monitored. Since the project operates in several island countries, technical, administrative, and financial information must flow between the project headquarters in St. Lucia, the Leeward and Windward Island Unit offices (St. Lucia and Antigua, respectively) and the individual countries. The project is also linked to CARDI headquarters in Trinidad.

An analysis of data and information flows within the FSR/D project was used to identify individual, specific requirements, and to design a network with hardware, software, and organizational components. The installation of hardware and the purchase of software is a relatively simple process; however, the training of individuals and the organization of people to form a functional human network is much more difficult. For this reason, the development of an installation procedure was considered an important element in the design of the network.

The network installation procedure was developed using the following assumptions: a) microcomputers should be viewed as tools to help efficiency; b) the timing of the installation of a microcomputer in an office is critical because it generates a surge of motivation that should be channeled into key project activities; c) training in the use of various software packages should occur in workshops where the emphasis is on the application (e.g., report writing, budgeting, analyzing experiments, etc.) and not on the computers; and d) the sequence in which software packages are introduced should begin with easier "user-friendly" packages with applications valuable to many staff and later proceed to more complex software valuable to only a few staff.

The key information and data processing needs of the FSR/D project were identified as:

1) <u>word processing capability</u> to make report writing more efficient and allow different studies to be electronically "cut-and-pasted" into different reports for various institutions that need to be kept informed of on-going activities;

2) <u>budgeting and financial management capabilities</u> to enable team leaders to estimate expenditures and monitor cash flows;

113

3) <u>statistical analysis capabilities</u> to allow country teams to do analyses currently done manually and to identify the types of analyses that should be done with assistance from the technical coordinators at the unit level or on the mainframe computer in Trinidad;

4) <u>data management capabilities</u> to integrate physical, biological, and socioeconomic data as the basis for the design of ongoing workplans and to communicate technological improvements to extension institutions; and

5) <u>communications capabilities</u> to transfer workplans, budgets, and reports to the project office and transfer data to technical unit offices and the project office for analysis.

THE FSR/D PROJECT MICROCOMPUTER NETWORK

In July, 1984, the South-East Consortium for International Development (SECID) was selected to provide technical assistance to the CARDI FSR/D project, and Marcus Ingle and Robert Hart became part of the technical assistance team. A SECID/CARDI/USAID workshop was held in Maryland to plan the technical assistance program. Specific time was allotted to plan the best way to design and implement the microcomputer network. Two computer specialists, Wayne Hinerman from Winrock, (a hardware specialist with extensive software expertise), and Ken Smith from the International Development Management Center of the University of Maryland, (a management specialist also with extensive software expertise), were invited to the workshop as consultants. CARDI was represented by Dr. Samsundar Parasram and Mr. Calixte George, the executive director and FSR/D project manager, respectively. A microcomputer network, described below, was designed and modified slightly after Hart moved to St. Lucia, Ingle completed a short-term assignment in Trinidad, and the procurement specialist of SECID (Harry Wheeler) visited IBM's regional office in Barbados.

<u>Hardware</u>: IBM and IBM-compatible microcomputers. IBM PC XTs were selected for Trinidad (CARDI headquarters) and St. Lucia (the FSR/D project headquarters), and IBM PCs were selected for each of the eight project islands. Later, it was learned that IBM could not provide service to five of the islands, and a decision was made to purchase Compaqs (IBM-compatible transportables) that could be shipped to the U.S. when maintenance was needed. Table 2.1 shows hardware installation and distribution throughout the network.

<u>Software</u>: WordStar and SuperCalc were selected to meet word processing and budgeting needs. The selection of a statistical package was deferred until CARDI biometricians could review the literature describing the more than forty available statistical packages. M-stat (developed by Michigan State University) and Sis-stat were borrowed so that they could be evaluated directly. Three Open Systems packages were selected to meet accounting needs. The selection of data management and communication software was deferred until later in the

project implementation process. Table 2.2 displays the software
selected and its distribution in the network.

<u>People/Organizational Components</u>: There were three types of
individuals linked within the network: a) users, b) user/coordinators,
and c) resource persons. The first group was composed of country team,
technical unit, and secretarial staff who used the microcomputer in
their work. The second group included individuals who, in addition to
using the computers to do their work, also coordinated, managed and
controlled the flow of accounting information, technical data, and
research reports. The resource group was composed of "experts" within
the project who were skilled in the use of specific software packages,
and available to respond to requests for assistance. A hardware and
operating system specialist was hired by CARDI, and two individuals in
the United States were asked to serve as "last resort" resources to be
contacted when technical assistance was needed.

Three types of information flowed through the CARDI microcomputer
network: a) financial and accounting information, b) technical data,
and c) reports. In the case of the FSR/D project, the accounting and
financial information flowed directly between the country teams and the
project office. The technical data and technical reports flowed from
the countries to the unit office and then to the project office. All
unit offices and the FSR/D project office are linked to CARDI headquarters in Trinidad. Not shown in the diagram are other project
offices that function below the unit or country levels.

INSTALLATION PHASES

The network was installed in phases for two reasons. First, CARDI's
institutional information and management capabilities were not
sufficient at the outset to operate the network. Installing the
network in phases (putting in part of the hardware and software) was
used as a motivator to quickly increase information management
capabilities. Second, a phased-in installation of the network allowed
corrections to be made in the network design.

The microcomputer network was installed in the following three phases:

1) <u>Initiation and Familiarization</u>: July 1984 – April 1985. In July
1984, the FSR/D project team leaders had their first contract to use
microcomputers as part of a workshop to develop the 1984–1985 workplans. The project budget was designed with a Supercalc spreadsheet by
asking each country team leader to enter the data for each line item in
their country budgets. The total budget was then calculated. One
microcomputer was installed at the project headquarters in August 1984
in St. Lucia. Staff began to use WordStar and Supercalc software.

TABLE 2.1

HARDWARE DISTRIBUTION IN THE CARDI MICROCOMPUTER NETWORK

CARDI Countries	CARDI Headquarters	CARDI Office	FSR/D Unit	Team
Trinidad Tobago	IBM XT			
St. Lucia		IBM XT	Compaq	IBM PC
Dominica				Compaq
St. Vincent				Compaq
Grenada				Compaq
Antigua			Compaq	IBM PC
St. Kitts/Nevis				Compaq
Monserrat				Compaq
Barbados		IBM PC		
Guyana		IBM XT		
Jamaica		IBM XT		
Belize		IBM XT		

In December 1984, two IBM XTs were installed, one in St. Lucia and one in Trinidad; and two Compaqs were installed, one in the Antigua unit office and one in the St. Vincent country team office. Printers did not arrive in Antigua and St. Vincent until January 1985. An applications workshop on report writing and budgeting was held in St. Lucia in December 1984 to coincide with the arrival of the first hardware shipment. All country team leaders and a secretary/administrative assistant from each island attended the workshop.

2) _Installation and Training_: April 1985 – April 1986. By April 1985, five additional Compaqs and three IBM PC's were installed on the remainder of the FSR/D project islands. In February and March 1985, the unit technical coordinators visited the islands and used their transportables to help country team leaders develop draft workplans. When the hardware arrived, country teams updated these plans and brought them to a planning workshop where they were consolidated into a project-level workplan and budget.

3) <u>Incremental Improvements and Further Training</u>: April 1986. By
April 1986, all hardware in the microcomputer network was installed in
all of the CARDI countries. Computers for Guyana, Jamaica, and Belize
are being purchased by projects other than the FSR/D project. A
proposal has been sent to IDRC to acquire modems for all of the
computers and to train staff in the use of communications software.
Using the experience acquired, an institutional-level data management
system will also be designed and implemented.

TABLE 2.2

SOFTWARE FOR CARDI FSR/D PROJECT

Name of Software	Description	Territories Installed
Accounts Payable	Open Systems accounting software	Trinidad St. Lucia
Advanced Diagnostics	Diagnostics disk for PC-XT	St. Lucia
CorrectStar	Efficient spelling checker for use with WordStar	St. Lucia
General Ledger	Open Systems accounting software	Trinidad St. Lucia
IBM Basic	Basic compiler	All CARDI micro territories
Mailmerge	Merge printing package for use with WordStar	Trinidad St. Lucia
Rm/Fortran	Fortran compiler	Trinidad
SpellStar	Spelling checker for use with WordStar	All CARDI micro territories
SuperCalc3	Spreadsheet	Trinidad St. Lucia
WordStar	Text editor	All CARDI micro territories

LESSONS FROM THE CARDI FSR/D PROJECT

The key lessons learned from the CARDI FSR/D Project experience include:

1) Involving project staff in the microcomputer network needs assessment and installation process influences the level of initial acceptability and continued use. In this case, a maximum staff involvement strategy was pursued from the outset with very favorable results.

2) Adoption of the use of microcomputer technology occurs most readily in a project management situation when the system is used in conjunction with high priority managerial and technical tasks that are routine and information-processing in nature.

3) Phased introduction of microcomputers beginning with relatively easy, individual uses and moving to multiple applications and networked uses appears to be a workable approach.

4) A learning-by-doing installation method is a feasible way to build staff competence and confidence on the microcomputer and simultaneously perform work-related information processing tasks.

APPLICATION #3:   INTRODUCTION OF MICROCOMPUTERS INTO CHOGORIA RURAL HOSPITAL AND COMMUNITY HEALTH PROGRAM (1)

Chogoria Hospital is a rural Presbyterian Church of East Africa (P.C.E.A.) hospital on the eastern side of Mt. Kenya. Although the nearest township is fifty kilometers away, the region is densely populated. Chogoria's catchment area holds 400,000 people. The hospital has 295 beds and accommodated 11,000 in-patients and 60,000 out-patients in 1985.

Chogoria also has a Community Health Department (CHD) which has thirty-three primary health care clinics. Last year over 250,000 individual clients were handled. Chogoria's CHD places strong emphasis on preventive medicine and is recognized for its successful family planning program which combines community-based distribution and clinic-based services. Chogoria boasts a 26 percent acceptance rate for family planning, well above the 8 percent national average. USAID/Kenya selected Chogoria to pilot a project with the objective of designing and implementing a microcomputer-based information system to improve family planning services. Final objectives included:

---

(1)   Thomas Carouso is Kenya Country Manager for Thunder and Associates, Inc. He has worked as microcomputer consultant and trainer for fourteen months during 1985-86 on this project.

1) An accounting system, with emphasis on the introduction of depart-
mental accountability, integration of the cash register receipts with
microcomputers, improved donor reporting capabilities, and improved
stock keeping systems;

2) An in-patient information system to track client admissions,
discharges, and diagnoses to improve hospital management as well as
provide a base for conducting analysis of patterns of illness in the
region;

3) Statistics on patient services provided by the thirty two field
clinics, to improve donor reporting and provide clinic extension
workers with accurate lists of family planning defaulters and at-risk
patients; and

4) Field entry of extensive evaluation survey data for several program
impact analysis studies.

The project's first phase ended in November 1985 and completed the
in-patient system, the Community Health Department Information System,
a redesigned chart of accounts, and training of hospital staff in all
of the above custom-designed applications and in the use of off-the-
shelf software for word processing, database applications, and
spreadsheets.

THE IN-PATIENT SYSTEM

<u>Activities</u>:

1) Evaluation of in-patient case sheet system and ward occupancy;

2) Determination of items to be tracked in system;

3) Design of system of daily reporting from wards to daily report
generation; and

4) Design of additional reports for conducting epidemiological
research and compilation of statistics for hospital annual report,
training on new manual system at in-patient admissions and at each of
the seven wards; programming of menu driven in-patient program, (i.e.,
data entry, report generation); training two staff members in
supervision of entire in-patient tracking system).

<u>Constraints</u>:

Initially, the daily manual reporting system from each of the seven
wards was often inaccurate. This was because many of the people
responsible for filling out the in-patient information sheets,
admissions books and discharge sheets were not involved in the entire
in-patient system and thus were not sensitive to the importance of
accurate reporting. In the past, inaccuracies went unnoticed. After
the key actors in the manual reporting process were shown the entire

system, including the computers, they became sensitive to the need for accurate, timely, and legible forms.

The in-patient system is currently working at Chogoria and is extremely successful. By 9:00 every morning the matron of the hospital receives a daily ward occupancy report which gives the number of patients in each ward, the number admitted and discharged from each ward, and the occupancy rate of each ward. This enables her to make effective and timely resource allocation decisions in distributing her nursing staff in the wards.

ACCOUNTING SYSTEM

An evaluation of the accounting system determined that before a computerized system could be implemented, the manual system would have to be totally redesigned including a departmentalized chart of accounts, consolidation and redesign of the storekeeping system, (there were previously seven separate stores), and the ability to track fixed assets. This redesign will facilitate the computerization of the accounts at Chogoria, a task to be completed as follow-on work.

Constraints:

Because of corruption in the storekeeping system, especially by certain powerful figures at the hospital, the stores had been separated into seven different units. This enabled the Community Health Department and the Nurses Training School to control their own stock supply. Various units resisted the consolidation process, not believing that there would be improved control and fearing that they would have to endure misuse, misallocation, etc., of the stores. This issue caused great debate and delayed the process of implementing the new accounting system.

The microcomputer forced a rationalization of the entire accounting process at Chogoria. This rationalization proved to be quite threatening, especially to those engaged in corruption. In addition, the anticipation of a computerized accounting system caused the accounting staff to worry about becoming redundant. It took a decided effort to convince the accounting staff that the new system would not take away jobs and would improve both the quality of their work and the management of the hospital.

THE COMMUNITY HEALTH DEPARTMENT INFORMATION SYSTEM

Activities:

1) Evaluation of existing donor reporting activities;

2) Evaluation of CHD referral system for prevention services, design of CHD information system based on reporting needs, desired improvements in management, and basis for conducting epidemiological analysis;

3) Design and preparation of training seminar for pilot group of clinics in use of new manual information system;

4) Preparation of training manuals for use of information systems;

5) Training seminar for pilot group of clinics;

6) Follow-up visit at pilot group clinic sites;

7) Design and prepare seminar for pilot group to evaluate and amend information system;

8) Change information system based on evaluation seminar;

9) Program information system including custom data entry screens with validation, utilities for editing day's work, saving to main file, conducting tape back-up, and report generation;

10) Train nurses at remaining clinics in use of information system;

11) Follow-up visits at all clinics using system; and

12) Train CHD staff in use of custom CHD computer program.

<u>Constraints:</u>

1) Difficulty in getting accurate information from clients visiting clinics;

2) Getting mid-level supervisory acceptance and support;

3) Introducing client card and numbering system;

4) Getting agreement on common or accepted village name and address in region;

5) Finding skilled persons to do data entry and supervision; and

6) Problems in informal power perceptions and change in roles among staff.

TRAINING

A large component of the project was training in word processing, spreadsheet use and design, and in basic database applications. Several members of the senior staff became quite involved, to the extent that they designed and programmed their own applications.

The following applications were designed for the project, and are
currently being utilized by staff who had never used a microcomputer
before this time.

Spreadsheet Applications

Cash and voucher accounts from clinics and dispensaries
Leprosy treatment accounts for donor reporting
Female sterilization records
Salary increase implications
Charitable donations recording
Dental unit accounting
Dental unit activity
Laboratory results

Word Processing

Most correspondence
Text merge with database of names and addresses for form letters
Mastertype: to improve typing skills
Other required documents

Database Applications

Each village is assigned a code, used in the in-patient and CHD systems
for demographic analysis.

Database tracking use of hospital vehicles
Database tracking tubal ligation operations
Database tracking interviewers and supervisors
Database tracking deliveries in Maternity Ward
Database tracking surgical theatre activities
Pharmaceutical tracking system
Salary database

HARDWARE/SOFTWARE REQUIREMENTS

Activities and Choices:

After the existing systems at Chogoria were evaluated and the designs
of the new systems from the senior staff were approved, software was
selected.   All the major systems required customization.   The CHD
system tracks 100,000 records per year with an average of twenty-two
characters per record.   Thus, it was necessary to use a database
program that could lend itself to customization and could accommodate
large amounts of data.   dBase III has proven to be a good choice for
this application.   Based on its ease of use, the word processing
package chosen was Volkswriter Deluxe; the spreadsheet program chosen
was Supercalc3; the statistical analysis package was StatPac, again
because of its ease of use.   MS-DOS is the only operating system that
can run these programs.   The large volume of data to be tracked
required use of hard disk systems with tape back-ups.

COMPAQ Deskpro 5's were chosen because:

o   they support MS-DOS;
o   the dealer in Nairobi was known to provide good service;
o   the dealer in Nairobi offered same-day maintenance or replacement of equipment, (a major attraction as Chogoria is three hours drive from Nairobi);
o   COMPAQ offered 30 megabyte hard disk systems for less money than the competition's 20 megabyte hard disk systems; and
o   COMPAQ's have a reputation for durability.

The voltage in Chogoria is very unstable. Although Kenya is supposed to be a 240V country, Chogoria averages about 205V. In addition, there are frequent black and brown-outs. Uninterruptable Power Supplies were procured to protect the equipment and allow the users to save their work during the frequent power fluctuations. Step-up transformers were used to increase the low voltage to 220V. NEC P3 printers were selected for their durability. They have proven to be workhorses.

LESSONS FROM THE CHOGORIA HOSPITAL PROJECT

1) Similar projects should always take voltage recorders to the project site for two weeks of analysis before any decisions on hardware and equipment back-up or protection are made. Although Kenya is a 240V country, 220V equipment would have been more appropriate for Chogoria.

2) The notion that humans are going to be replaced by computers has made its way to Chogoria. Only time and practice will show people involved with the systems that the microcomputer does not replace them, but makes their work better and more effective. This realization has finally reached the accounting office, where the staff once had tombstones in their eyes no matter how hard the "computer man" tried to convince them that they would not become redundant. One must be sensitive to this misconception.

3) Project workers must be sensitive to the profound effect of introducing microcomputers to Third World institutions. The power balance is disrupted. Individuals who show an interest and ability to work successfully with the machines are securing for themselves a position of prominence, not because they are related to powerful persons in the community, but because of their relative competence. This sudden rise is perceived as threatening, especially when the knowledge of the mysterious machine is not shared by everyone and not easily forfeited.

Similarly, management decisions are being made based on new criteria. In the past, when information was inaccurate, or more often, non-existent, decisions were made based on nepotism or whim. While it is easy to feel confident that the new set of decision-making criteria

being introduced are "better," it is important to tread gently. If key
actors are threatened, they will find ways to undermine the successful
use of such systems and maintain the traditional power structure. It
is essential to involve the key power personalities within the
administrative process so that the changes are perceived to be to their
benefit.

TABLE 3.1

MICROCOMPUTER APPLICATIONS DEVELOPED AT CHOGORIA HOSPITAL

```
 1.  Community Health Department Information System
     a. Family Planning
     b. Ante-Natal
     c. Child Welfare
     d. Community Based Distribution
 2.  In-Patient Tracking System
 3.  Transportation Database
 4.  Voluntary Surgical Contraception Spreadsheet
 5.  Tuberculosis Tracking System
 6.  Leprosy Tracking System
 7.  Clinic Accounting
 8.  Hospital Accounting
 9.  Drug/store Inventory
10.  Cash Handling
11.  Salaries Review
12.  Fees Review
13.  Laboratory
14.  Debtor/creditor List
15.  Word Processing (general correspondence, project proposals,
     meeting minutes)
16.  Staff Rotations
17.  Procedure Manual Editing
18.  Names and Addresses List
19.  Viva Survey Analysis
20.  Youth Programme Questionnaire Analysis
21.  Address Database
22.  Surgical Theatre Tracking
23.  Maternity Tracking
```

APPLICATION #4:   <u>COMPUTERIZATION OF THE NATIONAL BUDGET, MINISTRY OF</u>
<u>FINANCE AND PLANNING, KENYA</u> (1)

Late in 1981, Technical Assistance Advisors from Harvard Institute for
International Development (HIID) introduced microcomputers in the
Ministry of Agriculture and Livestock Development of Kenya to help with
expenditure monitoring. The results were so encouraging that
microcomputers were swiftly utilized in a number of other vital
financial management tasks in the Ministry of Finance and Planning
(MOFP). Efforts in computerizing the MOFP began in 1984 in clear
recognition of the success of this earlier application of microcomputers. In acknowledgement of the need for increased level of
effort, Thunder and Associates was hired to provide technical
assistance, purchasing, acquisition, and training. Since that time,
microcomputers have been used successfully in one complete budget
estimates cycle (i.e., Draft Budget, Forward Budget, and Revised
Budget). In addition, eighteen other key applications have been
computerized and thirteen others are planned for completion before
September, 1986. Over two hundred Ministry of Finance employees have
been trained in the use of computers and the computerized applications.

The National Budget of Kenya is not a single computer application but a
series of applications that interrelate in an information system. In
fact, many of the budget-related applications do not take place in the
same physical location. For instance, other ministries such as the
Ministry of Agriculture and Livestock Development, the Ministry of
Health, and the Office of the President are using microcomputers to
record their budget estimates while the Appropriation Accounts are
prepared at the Office of the Controller and Auditor General. This in
itself is an argument for the kind of decentralized, distributed
processing that microcomputers afford. But there are many other
reasons why microcomputers are the technology of choice. These
include:

1)   <u>Cost-Effectiveness</u>

Despite their proven track record, it is doubtful that microcomputers
would have been implemented in the MOFP had the ministry been forced to
pay for them. Fortunately, a management advisor from HIID was able to
secure a donation from Kaypro Corporation of ten microcomputers in May
of 1984. It was this donation that convinced key decision-makers
within the Ministry to accept the technology.

---

(1)   This case draws heavily from a series of reports and analyses by
Clay Wescott of Harvard Institute for International Development, Senior
Advisor to MOFP, and <u>The Budget for the Government of Kenya, Systems</u>
<u>and Computer Design</u> prepared for the Ministry of Finance, Kenya by
Ranel Covert and David Green.

2) <u>Superior Throughput</u>

One reason senior officials in MOFP have been so reluctant to accept
computerization is the less than optimal throughput experienced with
mainframe computers at the Government Computer Services Center (GCSC).
GCSC maintains two IBM mainframes (4331, 370/135) and a Wang VS 2200.
A recent study by UNDP (Herr: 1985) states that GCSC is several months
to several years behind in most applications.

The UNDP report on CBS found that manually prepared data was processed
more rapidly than computer processed data. The reasons given for the
setbacks were neglect, lack of priority given to applications, delays
in data entry, poor validation procedures, incomplete data files, an
outdated physical plant, and delays in printing. According to the
report, setbacks have become so profound that the problems in data
processing have begun to influence user demands on the system as well
as prioritizing of jobs.

3) <u>Ease of Use, Programmability, and Flexibility</u>

It is because of their relative ease of use and programmability that
microcomputers were successfully implemented in MOFP. Within a matter
of hours or days a novice user can be trained to enter data into a
database, compose documents on a word processor, or construct simple
spreadsheets. There are thousands of cheap and available software
packages for the microcomputers, and those in the Ministry are
experiencing constant use because of the flexibility that this allows.
Even machines that are dedicated to the budget are sometimes used for
word processing, spreadsheets for analysis, and other applications.

4) <u>Portability, Distributed Processing, District Focus</u>

Compared with mainframe or minicomputers, microcomputers are highly
portable. This is a very important characteristic given the
distributed data processing tasks that compose the budget. For
example, much of the estimates preparation cycle should logically take
place within individual ministries. Decentralized processing implies
returning information processing responsibilities back to the
ministries. This would allow each ministry to monitor and influence
its budget.

Of importance in the implementation of microcomputers is their impact
on the District Focus program for rural development, initiated in 1984
by the Office of the President. In terms of data processing, District
Focus places great demands on Government's ability to provide timely,
relevant information. According to Treasury Circular Number 5, the
national budget is a compilation of requests and estimates from the
districts. Thus, the information loop should look like this:

Ideal Information Flow

```
Districts------------>Ministries----------->Treasury
         ^                       ^                      |
         |                       |                      |
         -----------------------------------------------
```

District level planning means enabling the districts to influence the ministries in setting development priorities. In the past, Budget information was not disaggregated in time to make it back to the district levels. Once the implementation of microcomputers has been fully completed in the ministries and in the districts, then this extremely important information loop will be closed.

Recent policy measures undertaken by the Kenyan Government are strongly focused on decentralization. This type of focus allows target populations the most influence, and the most responsibility for their economic well-being. Along with this move toward decentralization comes the fact that the economy of the government sector in each individual province in Kenya is now more complex than that of the entire country in 1964.

Clearly, a computer system of some sort is needed to facilitate this process. But such a computer system cannot be based on a central mainframe which breaks down or suffers serious data processing bottlenecks. In addition, the recurrent costs of hooking up terminals to a mainframe or minicomputer, via direct connect or modem, are prohibitive. This is especially true in light of the fact that ministries and officers are always changing their locations.

Microcomputers offer redundancy and the potential for standardization; and, more importantly, they mesh well with Kenya's efforts to decentralize to the district levels.

The following is a more extensive illustration of the Budget Information System, showing both the geographical location and name of some of the processes which compose the budget.

BUDGET INFORMATION SYSTEM

The Budget of Kenya is a complex process serving many functions. As an information system the Budget can be conceived in four major cycles. Much of the following is taken from the <u>Guide to the Government of Kenya Budgetary Process</u>, produced for the Ministry of Finance by a member of the HIID team in June 1985.

Ceilings Preparation Cycle: In this phase, officials in the Treasury (principally the Budget Supply Department and the Macro Planning Unit) derive appropriate spending ceilings for each vote given the calculation of total projected revenue and expenditures for a given financial year.

Estimates Preparation Process: This phase is composed of three parts:

1)   <u>Program Review and Forward Budget</u> – The annual <u>Forward Budget</u> exercise should take place in July and August of the new financial year for all ministries and is led by the Permanent Secretary to the Treasury. Taking the program targets and the five-year Forward Budget of the National Development Plan as the basic frame of reference, the program content of ministry programs is revised in light of current structural problems of the economy (such as the increased need to create more employment or problems with the balance of payments).

In this exercise, ministries are required to prepare program briefs indicating program changes since publication of the Plan and program adjustments in response to new economic guidelines in the Treasury Circular. In addition, at least a three-year draft forward budget must be submitted indicating the ministries' revised forward requirements for both their Recurrent and Development Budgets. Ceilings that have been approved by Cabinet are used to guide this process. This material is screened and discussed by the relevant Estimates Working Groups (EWGs), which pass their recommendations on to the Budgetary Procedures Group (BPG).

<u>The Forward Budget Product</u> – Before computerization, final printouts of the forward budget were not available. Indeed, preparation and discussion of the forward budget did not occur in a timely fashion. With the advent of microcomputers, the forward budget was produced and printed for distribution. Thus, the forward budget has become the important planning instrument that it was designed to be.

2)   <u>Revised and Supplementary Estimates</u> – The purpose of the annual **Revised Estimates** is to enable the operating ministries and the Treasury to revise the budget of the current financial year as published in the Printed Estimates and to reallocate public funds based on progress in physical implementation, incurring of actual expenditure, and collection of revenue. Revised Estimates are important to the Government for identifying trends of actual costs, expenditure, and revenue, for re-adjusting priorities, and for forecasting the future impact of on-going commitments. Operating ministries are usually required to submit their Revised Estimates, together with explanatory notes, in November/December for the purpose of screening by the Estimates Working Groups and the Budgetary Procedures Group. Supplementary funds above and beyond those reallocated may then be voted by Parliament early in the calendar year.

<u>The Revised Estimates Product</u> – The product for the Revised Estimates is composed of two documents which are forwarded to the Parliament for approval early in the calendar year. These

printed documents (one for Recurrent, and one for Development)
give an account of real expenditure history as well as detailed
explanations of variances between planned and actual
expenditures or receipts.

3) <u>Draft Annual Estimates</u> — The third stage of annual estimates
preparation cycle is concerned with the <u>Draft Annual Estimates</u>
for the following financial year. The rough ceilings for that
financial year were already set during the Forward Budget
exercise, which took place earlier in the current financial
year. These ceilings are updated within the Ministry of
Finance and Planning and are sent out when a call for estimates
is made through another Treasury Circular, ideally issued in
December for the next financial year's <u>Draft Annual Development
and Recurrent Estimates</u>.

<u>The Draft Estimates Product</u> — This is the most important legal
document produced by the Treasury. By law, the Draft Annual
Estimates **must** be presented to Parliament before the start of
the Fiscal Year (July 1st). Failure to do so in the past has
exacted many costs, not the least of which was the firing of
Treasury officials responsible for this product. It was the
computerization of this product, first produced by
microcomputers for the Draft Budget exercise in March through
June 1985, which convinced Treasury planners to computerize the
whole of the Budget process.

Expenditure Cycle: The operating ministries may incur expenses on or
before the time that the Parliament approves the new Draft Annual
Recurrent and Development Estimates. Careful monitoring of these
expenses is essential to the Budget process. Problems of underex-
penditure are just as serious as those relating to overexpenditure.

The Ministry of Finance and Planning has initiated a series of
microcomputer applications designed to replace manual expenditure and
receipt monitoring methods. These include:

1) <u>Paymaster General Account</u> — This is essentially a record of the
Government's checking account at the Central Bank of Kenya. Reports
from this application include a monthly trial balance of all
ministries, and a daily record of their transactions with the CBK.

2) <u>Imprest System</u> — The Imprest is an expense account system for all
officers in the operating ministries. The Imprest System is designed
to keep a running balance of all qualified officers for the use of
Imprest monies.

3) <u>Public Debt</u> — The Public Debt System is designed to provide
up-to-date information on all external loans. This will enable decision makers within the Government of Kenya to know the amounts they
must reserve for servicing these loans, and how much money they can
rely on for any given Fiscal Year.

4) <u>The Votebook System</u> — The Votebook is a computerized ledger system. Each vote (i.e., Ministry) must keep a record of expenditures on budgeted items. The Votebook is designed to provide a cumulative balance of monies spent on every item, as well as a declining balance of the monies that are available to expend on those items.

These applications, once successfully implemented in the Ministry of Finance and Planning, will be a vital source of input for budget planners. In addition, since all operating ministries maintain manual accounting systems similar to the ones described above, it is most probable that these computerized systems will become the prototypes for computerized Expenditure Cycle monitoring in the ministries. This is especially true since it is the Ministry of Finance which is responsible for the computerization of all operating ministries.

Analysis and Audit Cycle: At the close of the Fiscal Year, the Office of the Controller and Auditor General conducts an evaluation and audit of every vote in the Government of Kenya. Using the printed budget estimates as a source, the Controller and Auditor General issues a review called <u>The Appropriation Accounts, Other Accounts, and the Accounts of the Funds for the Year</u>. This document is a compilation of reports which explain in great detail the government's financial status. The Ministry of Finance has provided computers, programs, and training for the C&AG's office so that they can produce their report in a more timely fashion. In the past the Appropriation Accounts has been up to a year out of date.

<u>Analysis</u> — This is, of course, one of the most important parts of the Budget process. So far, computerization has afforded more analysis than was previously possible. For example, on July 8, 1985, a World Bank mission visiting Kenya requested an analysis of the 1985/86 Estimates by item group. Using the microcomputers a ministry staff member was able to provide them with their report in two days. Although such an exercise would be possible in theory to complete manually, it would have taken weeks or months of effort. Still, proper analysis of the Budget data remains a largely unexplored region. The potential for computerized analysis is great and the potential impacts of this analysis on future budgets even greater.

LESSONS FROM THE MOFP NATIONAL BUDGET

1) Complex large-scale applications such as an entire national budget process can be done using microcomputer technology.

This conclusion follows from the successful work to date, again demonstrating that microcomputers have the capability to do what was previously seen as a mini or mainframe application. Using microcomputers to do routine and high priority applications is proving preferable to the larger computers.

2) Host country personnel are proving ready, willing, and able to
learn microcomputer technology.

The staff of the ministry have demonstrated the ability to learn to use
microcomputers for data entry, programming, and general use with a
minimum of learning and training time as compared to working with
larger computer systems. Access to the microcomputer has provided the
incentive for people to work with the technology.

3) The unavailability of service, maintenance and parts can prove to
be a major impediment, if not provided for in the project.

The ability to support the equipment with service and maintenance has
been a continuing concern. The importation of equipment and parts
because of local unavailability has been time-consuming. The situation
is improving as the technology becomes more available in the general
marketplace and the government changes its perception toward the import
of technology.

4) The middle managers and decision-makers have readily adapted to the
increased availability of information.

Introduction of any new procedure within an organization is generally
met with resistance, and the MOFP is no exception. However, the level
of resistance is not unusually high but rather the norm for any
organizational development change of similar magnitude. As the
microcomputer has addressed a concrete concern, i.e., the production of
the national budget on a timely basis, the level of resistance has not
been as severe as it would have been for a less tangible product.

6) The need to plan the introduction of microcomputer systems in any
organization increases as the level of effort or applications undertaken increases.

Introducing microcomputers in an ad hoc manner for large-scale
endeavors increases mid- and upper-level management resistance. The
introduction of microcomputers must be seen as a major organizational
effort to be seriously planned and coordinated to avoid the
disorientation that follows from too rapid change.

7) The demand for microcomputer availability within an organization
grows at a rate directly proportional to organizational access.

The use of the microcomputer by professional staff and managers can be
assumed to grow if they are exposed to its potential. This must be
taken into consideration regarding training of staff and scheduling
access and use of the systems by others.

TABLE 4.1

THE MOFP BUDGET INFORMATION SYSTEM

CYCLE	APPLICATIONS	STATUS
1) Ceilings Preparation	Budget Out-Turn (IMF/MOF)	1
	Revenue Estimates	1
	Import License Tax	1
	Actual Import Schedule	1
	Tariff Rate Changes	1
	National Cereals Cash Flow	1
	Cereals Shipment	1
	Compendium of Donor Project	1
	Donor Disbursement Reports	1
	Econometric Model Simulations	1
	Sales Tax Revenue	4
	Revenue Forecasting	4
2) Estimates Preparation	Forward Budget	1
	Revised Budget	1
	Draft Budget	1
3) Expenditure	Votebook	2
	PayMaster General	3
	Imprest	3
	Public Debt	3
	Exchequer Returns	1
	KIDRES	4
	Parastatal Accounts	4
	Financial Institutions	4
	Donor Briefs	4
4) Analysis & Audit	Appropriation Accounts	1
	Item Group Analysis	1
	IMF Monitoring Program	1
	Rural Infrastructure	1
	Comparative Analysis	4

LEGEND -- 1) Completed/Functional
2) Completed/Not yet implemented
3) Design complete/Programming begun
4) Not yet designed

APPLICATION #5:   <u>TRAINING PEACE CORPS VOLUNTEERS FOR THE PEACE CORPS/THAILAND KAYPRO PROJECT</u> (1)

In October 1985 twenty-seven Peace Corps volunteers (PCVs) were trained to use five packaged software programs. In May and June of 1986 approximately 20 additional volunteers were trained. Participation by the volunteers in The Peace Corps Thailand Kaypro Project meant a commitment to an innovative microcomputer effort. Six Kaypro 2 microcomputers were placed at six sites throughout Thailand and are being used by PCVs to develop applications relevant to their assignments. This is the first group of Peace Corps volunteers ever trained to use packaged software and introduce microcomputer technology to counterparts within local government offices, staff at the sites, and other PCVs.

The criteria for a volunteer's acceptance in the training program were based on interest and availability, not experience. The software packages used for training were the ones that came with the computer. This discussion describes the project history, training process, and installation. Peace Corps/Thailand is now responsible for sustaining project activities.

PROJECT HISTORY

Work on the "Kaypro Project" began in 1983 when PC/Thailand received an inquiry from PC/Washington about its interest in receiving one free Kaypro computer for volunteer use. Peace Corps/Thailand accepted, but the five other Peace Corps offices in the region declined. The Peace Corps Training Officer suggested PC/Thailand ask for all six machines. PC/Washington was positive but wanted a proposal describing the project--how it would be organized and what the volunteers would be expected to do. First the Peace Corps Director discussed the idea with the Director General of the Department of Technical and Economic Cooperation (DTEC), other officials of the Royal Thai Government, and the Director of USAID. All were enthusiastic. Then he worked with USAID officials to choose USAID project sites that would support the purchase of peripherals and pay for a consultant to do the training. The Peace Corps volunteers were then surveyed to determine their level of experience and interest. Their experience was good and their interest was great.

Using Royal Thai Government, USAID and volunteer interest and experience as the rationale, a proposal describing the project was submitted to PC/Washington in April 1984. Unfortunately, during the time that PC/Washington and Kaypro were considering the proposal, the main USAID project (which was to pay for two sets of peripherals and

---

(1)   Marcia Hamilton was the Project Manager for The Department of Technical and Economic Cooperation of the Royal Thai Government in a joint effort with the United States Peace Corps, the United States Agency for International Development, and the Kaypro Corporation.

the consultants) was completed. Thus, when the proposal was accepted there was no clear funding mechanism for the peripherals (printers, diskettes, power supplies, etc.) or the consultants. USAID, still committed to working with Peace Corps, located two additional projects in which to place the Kaypros and decided to use $37,500 from the Emerging Problems of Development Project (EPDII).

In May 1985, the Peace Corps was informed that the funds had been transferred to the Department of Technical and Economic Cooperation (DTEC), which would administer the project. Until that time, it had been understood that the USAID would give funds directly to Peace Corps. This change in project management function caused new delays in setting up contracts for the consultants to manage the project and for contracting the ordering of peripherals and supplies. Contracts were finalized in July 1985. In August, most of the peripherals and supplies were ordered. The printers required to print Thai characters came from Japan. Ordering them was delayed until a waiver was granted to order equipment that was not made in the United States.

THE PROJECT OBJECTIVES

The main objective of the Peace Corps/Thailand Kaypro Project was to respond to the Royal Thai Government's focus on technology by providing a cadre of volunteers trained to act as catalysts in introducing micro-computer technology.

The underlying objectives were:

1) To improve organizational efficiency and effectiveness in the areas of reporting, record-keeping, accounting, scheduling, data analysis, and communication;

2) To diffuse microcomputer technology, applications, and learning to local rural development organizations;

3) To provide volunteers with a viable new skill critical to their future work in development or other fields;

4) To accept Kaypro's offer of six Kaypro microcomputers only if they were Kaypro 2's, 4's, or 10's (because only they—not the Kaypro II—have the graphics mode necessary for Thai software). To provide peripheral equipment (uninterruptable power supply, supplies, diskettes, furniture, dust covers, temperature control devices) through linkages with USAID;

5) To select five appropriate projects throughout Thailand where five Peace Corps microcomputers would be placed for access by a group of trained volunteers, and to place the sixth Kaypro at the Peace Corps Office in Bangkok;

6) To select a total of thirty-six volunteers with experience and/or interest in microcomputers who were located within working distance of

each of the five microcomputer sites and of the Peace Corps Office in
Bangkok, the sixth site. To qualify, the volunteers needed to have at
least one year of service left when they completed the survey;

7) To fund the peripherals, one Project Manager and one Project
Assistant; this would be done with USAID monies to be administered by
the Department of Technical and Economic Cooperation of the Royal Thai
Government;

8) To train a cadre of PCV trainers/catalysts/application developers
on Kaypro equipment and software, including Thai software;

9) To develop, test, and produce "how to" documentation on local level
applications (in Thai and English) for skill and technology transfer
and possible Peace Corps worldwide replicability; and

10) In cooperation with PC/Washington, to determine whether this
microcomputer pilot project justified consideration of recruitment of
microcomputer volunteers for specific assignments.

The project was designed so that each trained Peace Corps Volunteer
worked with one (or more) software programs at the Kaypro site nearest
his/her assignment site. The volunteer was responsible for:

o   using one or more of the packaged software programs to
    produce an application relevant to the assignment;

o   producing a short manual in English and in Thai about
    the application so that project site staff and/or other
    Peace Corps volunteers can sustain the effort; and

o   training a project site and/or counterpart staff member
    to use one or more of the software programs provided
    --either to do the PCV application or another relevant
    application.

THE PEACE CORPS KAYPRO TRAINING PROGRAM

The Peace Corps Training Office provided support for two six-day
training sessions. Although more than forty volunteers were eligible
for training, scheduling restrictions made it possible to train only
twenty-seven volunteers in October 1985. Training was provided for two
groups in English word processing, data retrieval, spreadsheet
analysis, Thai word processing, and the use of CP/M. This took place
in one large room at the Vienthai Hotel in Bangkok. Six "sites" lined
the perimeter of the room and tables filled the middle. Three trainees
were assigned to each computer "site" according to their program
(engineering, plant protection, malaria, etc.) Each "site" was
equipped with a computer, training materials and documentation, a log,
a sign-up sheet, an Uninterruptable Power Supply (UPS), and three of
the "sites" had printers. Every day began with a review of the
previous day and a preview of the day to come; it ended with processing

the particular software package that had been introduced that day.
Discussions involved problems and "insights" into each package.
Flipcharts were posted for trainees to note "Equipment, WordStar,
CalcStar, DataStar and CP/M insights." The trainees were checked out
on each program to ensure that they could access the program, do basic
procedures, save their work, and leave the program.

STRUCTURE OF THE TRAINING PROGRAM

The training program was designed to simulate the reality that Peace
Corps volunteers would face in the field. This included troubleshooting and solving problems with access, equipment, loss of
information, disk security, and record keeping.

Each computer was coded 1-6 and each had a sign-up sheet, a log, a
Training Manual, and accompanying documentation. Volunteers used the
sign-up sheet to plan computer access during the afternoon and evening,
and the log was used to record what they did.

Because the C-Itoh printers had not been ordered until two weeks before
the training, printers had to be borrowed. There were not enough to go
around and there was only one printer that printed Thai. Therefore, a
printing schedule had to be established.

Each trainee received two diskettes--one to use as a data diskette and
one as a copy. Volunteers learned to format and copy on the first day
of training and were expected to have two identical diskettes at all
times. (Several people learned their lesson the hard way by losing
data.)

Each volunteer received a "Reference Manual" that included a project
history, project and training objectives, training schedule, software
program glossaries, and several blank pages for notes. One sixty-page
"Computer Training Manual"--instructions for the five software programs
(CP/M, WordStar, DataStar, CalcStar and ThaiStar)--were available at
each machine. In addition, resource materials were placed on reserve
for evening reading.

Volunteers were expected to spend from 8:30 in the morning until 4:00
in the afternoon each day for six days, learning one new program a day
and participating in one discussion relevant to the project. The
computer room was open from 4:00 until 10:00 each night with at least
one consultant available at all times. (Some nights trainees stayed
until 3:00 in the morning.) The volunteers needed to spend at least
two hours alone on each program before being introduced to it and four
hours developing an application--fourteen hours minimum. The average
number of hours spent by trainees was 15.8; however, those who became
most proficient spent from twenty-three to forty hours.

During training, users' groups were formed by geographical area and a
Site Leader was selected to manage access. A PeaceKUG (Peace Corps
Kaypro User's Group) was formed to share insights gained at the Kaypro

sites as well as describe applications. One volunteer was selected as
the PeaceKUG Newsletter editor. Application development policy was
discussed and initial access management procedures established. During
training, volunteers also produced an application relevant to their
assignments and planned ways to expand and revise their applications.

Trainees produced applications that were either something they would
continue to work with or something they needed or wanted to do that
could be done in a day. There were fifteen CalcStar, four DataStar,
five WordStar and three ThaiStar applications produced during training
as a prelude to applications to be produced for assignments. The
applications were:

CALCSTAR--<u>Spreadsheet</u>: Rice pest control data; results of parasite
surveys; computing class grades; cost estimates for engineering
project; monthly slide positive rate by jungwat (province); 4-H
activities by Amphur (county); 4-H project budget; project construction
budget; concrete cost estimate for spillway of particular design; feed
formulations for chickens and swine with four variables; class
averages; livestock ratio formulas; mosquito net project control sheet
and budget.

DATASTAR--<u>Record Retrieval System</u>: Records on PC volunteers assigned to
Department of Agriculture; pharmacy inventory control records; PCV
engineering project records; fish production survey.

WORDSTAR--<u>English Word Processing</u>: Price list for engineering supplies;
program form for pests and diseases; small project proposal; hand-out
on requirements for first-year English; hand-out on farming terraced
land.

THAISTAR--<u>Thai/English Word Processing Program</u>: CP/M instructions in
Thai; introduction to Thai bureaucracy; list of medicinal herbs in Thai
and English.

AT THE SITE

One Kaypro microcomputer was installed at each of the following sites:
The Non-formal Education Center in Lampao, Kalasin; The Northeast
Regional Office of Agriculture Center, Khon Kaen; the Regional Non-
Formal Education Center in Lampang; the National Association of the
Deaf in Thailand, Bangkok; The Department of Technical and Economic
Cooperation, Bangkok; and the Peace Corps Office, Bangkok. These sites
were appropriate because the projects:

o   needed volunteers to provide microcomputer training and
     develop applications at the local level;

o   provided volunteers with access to the microcomputer;
     and

o   were located in the northeast, north, central parts of
     Thailand.

During installation, one day was devoted to actually setting up the
equipment and the next was set aside for volunteers to formally meet
Kayprosite staff, schedule access for the next month, and review
software if necessary. When the equipment was installed, volunteers
and Kayprosite staff had access to the following microcomputer system:

 1 Kaypro Microcomputer modified for Thai and English
 1 Datasaver 90 Watt Uninterruptable Power Supply
 5 printer ribbons
10 boxes of diskettes (10 diskettes per box)
 1 Kaypro dust cover
 1 C-Itoh printer modified for Thai
 1 C-Itoh printer dust cover
 1 floppy disk container
 1 box of 2,000 sheets of computer paper 9" x 11"
 1 box of 2,000 sheets of computer paper 11" x 15"
   Appropriate cables, plugs, adapters and fuses

Volunteers received the revised "Training Manual," and the site
received documentation that included both reference and training guides
for WordStar, DataStar, Supersort, CalcStar, CP/M and MBasic.   The
software available with the computer included a set of masters and two
sets of working copies (produced during training) of the following:
THAISTAR; CP/M Version 2.2; DATASTAR, SUPERSORT, and CALCSTAR; THE WORD
PLUS; WORDSTAR and MAILMERGE; PROFIT PLAN; MICROSOFT BASIC-80.

COMPUTER USE AT KAYPROSITES

Computer use at individual Kayprosites is the result of reports submitted by Group Leaders based on time entered in the logs at each site.
From January through March 1986, the PCVs and Thai Staff used the five
Kayprosite computers for a total of 823.75 hours.   This averages
approximately 55 hours per month per site over the three months since
installation.   PCVs used the machines for 342 hours compared to 481.75
hours of Kayprosite staff and co-worker use.   (Thus, PCVs used the
machines approximately 41.5% of the time and Thai staff used the equipment 58.5% of the time.)   PCVs generally use the computer on weekends
and staff use it during the week. It is important to note that,
although the computers are well-used, volunteers might use the equipment more in the future. They state that they have not had sufficient
time to fully incorporate microcomputer activities into their lives.

During Phase I, a two-person training team monitored the project, did
troubleshooting, conducted follow-up visits, and created applications
and materials. As of April 1, 1986 the project was turned over to
Peace Corps/Thailand.   From now on--Phase II--PC/Thailand is responsible for continuing to train new PCVs to replace those completing
their service and for monitoring the development and completion of
applications.   Once a software application is completed, the volunteer

submits it (on disk) as well as a short manual in Thai and English, to
the Peace Corps office in Bangkok.

LESSONS FROM PEACE CORPS/THAILAND KAYPRO PROJECT

1) It is possible to introduce five packaged software programs to a
large group, one program a day over six days, without overloading and
confusing trainees.

2) It is possible to train three people at one computer if they work
as a team and schedule individual time.

3) It is possible for trainees to learn packaged software programs
well enough in one day to then select a program to produce and print an
application relevant to their work.

4) When training people to use microcomputers, it is effective to mix
hands-on sessions with sessions designed to discuss the issues
surrounding the use of microcomputers as development tools, system
management, access, and other host-country concerns.

5) Even though a host-country government is committed to technological
advancement, government procedures for acquiring microcomputer
equipment (as well as duties and taxes) often have not been changed to
reflect this commitment; concomitant delays are unavoidable.

6) A complex and innovative project involving the interaction of three
agencies (The Royal Thai Government, the United States Agency for
International Development, the United States Peace Corps) and one
corporation (The Kaypro Corporation) will necessarily include delays,
as all the bureaucracies must establish new guidelines and procedures.

7) When the organization and management structure of the original
proposal was no longer applicable, the proposal should have been
rewritten to establish new, clear lines of responsibility and
authority.

8) The original USAID plan to directly fund the Peace Corps to
administer the Kaypro Project would have made the administration of
this project easier.

9) The Directors at the Kayprosites are pleased to have both the
computer systems and Thai-speaking PCVs with whom to work.

These Peace Corps volunteers are the first volunteers to be trained to
act as catalysts in diffusing microcomputer technology. Such an effort
must consider the implications and issues surrounding microcomputers in
the Thai culture--especially in areas where there is a marked contrast
between the work done by rice farmers and the work done by computer
advocates. Questions will be raised and answers sought. It will be up
to those who use and teach microcomputer skills to develop applications
that are meaningful in the Thai development context.

Volunteers in Technical Assistance (VITA) is a private, nonprofit organization that gives technical assistance in developing countries. It offers information aimed at helping people and groups select and implement technologies appropriate to their situations. Emphasis is on small- and medium-scale technologies in the fields of renewable energy, agriculture and food processing, water supply and sanitation, housing and construction, and small business development.

In cooperation with the Radio Amateur Satellite Corporation (AMSAT), VITA is developing the PACSAT low earth orbit satellite system as a global technical information exchange network. PACSAT is designed to provide fast, high quality, reliable information transfer to, from, and among developing countries. The PACSAT technology addresses applications that are currently not easily supported by the existing international telecommunications infrastructure.

The satellite will be able to receive a message from any point in the world, hold it, and deliver it to any other point in the world. The ground equipment needed--including the antenna--will fit inside a briefcase, will be battery-powered and should cost less than $2,000 to manufacture in small quantities. A prototype, already in orbit, was built by VITA and AMSAT volunteers and integrated into a spacecraft constructed by the University of Surrey (England) and launched by NASA in 1984.

Most mini and mainframe computers, as well as microcomputers, have a provision for electronic mail which uses the data storage capability of the computer to save a message so it can be retrieved later by others. Some computers are linked together and pass messages between them, so that users of one computer can leave messages for users of another. This is done by linking computers or by leaving messages on a central computer called a "mailbox" or a "bulletin board." PACSAT would eventually function as such a bulletin board.

PACSAT, currently under development for a launch by the Space Shuttle sometime in 1987, will use a mode called "packet radio" as its primary access system. Packet radio is not new, but is just beginning to see wide use by amateur and commercial radio systems.

---

(1) Gary Garriott is Manager of Information Technology at Volunteers in Technical Assistance. He holds a Ph.D. in Social Technology from the Union Graduate School (Cincinnati, Ohio).

In its simplest form, packet radio connects one computer to another via radio for error-free data communication. A device called a "terminal node controller" (TNC) formats the message into small sections called "packets" and uses a radio to transmit it at high speed. At the same time, the TNC "listens" to the radio and sends received messages to your computer. TNCs are available today at prices below $200. The destination station confirms the correct reception of each packet by transmitting a short acknowledgement. Although this sounds complicated, the tasks of formatting packets, adding address and error-check codes, transmitting, retransmitting, acknowledging and monitoring are done by the TNC. The computer simply sends and receives data in the same way it would if it were connected to a standard telephone modem. All of the complex functions are "transparent" to the user.

The importance of breaking data into small individually addressed packets is spectrum efficiency. With packet radio, you can use the same frequency at the same time as many other stations. You simply insert your packets between others' packets. Each station's unique address keeps the messages separate. The error detection and acknowledgement procedures prevent two stations from transmitting simultaneously.

PACSAT will pass over any point on the earth at least four times a day, and will be in sight of any given location for an average of ten minutes each pass. When PACSAT is in sight, a ground station can transmit messages for storage in PACSAT's memory and/or retrieve messages from PACSAT's memory. Operation will be automatic, i.e., operators need not be present to send or retrieve messages.

The disadvantage of a store-and-forward message system such as PACSAT is time: you can only send and receive messages at certain times of the day or night. Because the spacecraft is actually carrying your message from you to the destination, a message can be delayed by zero minutes to 10.5 hours.

Because PACSAT is optimized for slow, short, and sporadic messages and because low cost and portability of the ground stations are of prime concern, the time and rate problem is not important. This line of reasoning is known as matching the application to the resource or turning bugs into features.

PACSAT will be built mainly by volunteer labor and estimates of its cost are less than $1 million. Although contributions have been received from Tektronix, the Hoover Foundation and USAID, additional funding from public- and private-sector sources is required to allow the project to continue.

EQUIPMENT

A PACSAT ground station will consist of a microcomputer, a terminal node controller, and a radio. The user will store messages in the computer, and the messages will be automatically relayed to PACSAT when

the satellite comes into range. The computer will also query PACSAT to
see if any messages are waiting for it. Messages are then downloaded
from PACSAT to the computer.

When used by amateurs in developed countries, the computer can be any
size and left on at all times. When built to be carried into the
field, the computer and radio will be as small as possible. The
station will operate from solar-charged batteries and be briefcase-
sized. The computer, using information fed into it regarding its
current location and information about PACSAT's orbit available from
PACSAT itself, will be able to initiate communication when PACSAT is
about to come into range.

As this is being written, extensive experimentation of the PACSAT
prototype store-and-forward message system is about to begin on the
UoSAT-2 satellite. VITA has installed its own ground station and
plans to communicate with other stations in the network as well as
install demonstration stations at selected foreign locations. UoSAT-2
uses amateur radio frequencies which are ideal for experimentation and
demonstration purposes.

LESSONS FROM PACSAT SATELLITE COMMUNICATION PROJECT

1) A project always takes longer than originally anticipated.

2) As of press time, the future of the Space Shuttle mission is
uncertain. Other launch possibilities are being investigated.

3) The reliance on volunteer labor creates logistical/organizational
issues, many of which can be addressed by linking the group through
electronic mail (which PACSAT will someday replace) and other means,
such as face-to-face meetings, to maintain morale and interest. A paid
manager to coordinate the work of volunteers is indispensable.

4) It is difficult to obtain funding, even from donors who en-
thusiasticly support the concept.

5) There is a place in development for low-cost digital forms of
communication. However, implementing these systems may require comple-
ments to the existing international telecommunications infrastructure.
PACSAT is an example of such low-cost innovative solutions to pressing
needs in development.

APPLICATION #7:   <u>NEEDS ASSESSMENT IN PAKISTAN</u> (1)

As part of a large-scale foreign assistance project conducted for the National Institute of Public Administration in Lahore, Pakistan, two consultants were asked to conduct a "needs assessment" to help restructure a training program for senior Pakistani civil service personnel. This needs assessment included interviews with a cross-section of relevant Pakistani government staff, the actual participants in the training program, and the staff of the institution where the training would take place. Based upon this assessment a revitalized training program would be designed and carried out some weeks later.

A concern of the technical assistance (expatriate) project director was the difficulty in getting important Pakistani officials to base institutional development policy decisions on real data about performance and needs. Therefore, needs assessments were conducted prior to any interventions or direct institutional support activities. Several such assessments had been conducted for related training design purposes before the case in point. The informality of documenting these assessments made their longer term and strategic usefulness very limited.

The needs assessment for the civil service training program was done with the aid of a small lapsize portable computer. A more general database of material was developed to support larger policy decisions in collaboration with Pakistan government officials. The portable lapsize computer was used to enter notes and interviews from the field for short reports, and later transferred electronically into a more flexible text database management system.

Twenty-five people were interviewed in several different cities. Two trips were made to rural areas for meetings with locally elected village government members whose input was very important to the substance of the training program under revision. Notes were taken on paper in all interviews, and these notes were entered into the portable computer later each day or evening. This was done by one of the consultants who shared the results with the other for revisions, corrections, and additions daily.

A typical interview session, as reflected in the computerized notes, would contain between fifteen and twenty-five separate one or two sentence "items" that captured an important point made in the inter-view. These items, along with key terms and identifying information would form the data in the text database being developed. For example, one item reads: "Many feel there must be a rural development policy

---

(1) Tom Armor is an Organization Development consultant working extensively overseas. He has great interest in computer technology in support of social and behavioral change efforts. His doctorate from UCLA is in Behavioral Science for Management.

statement to guide them. Such a statement will be difficult to find, perhaps it has to be evolved by each for himself." The comment is referenced by interviewee name and position, as well as such key terms as National Office (vs. Provincial or Local), Rural Development, Policy, and individual.

The interview data is now available as a text database, allowing easy retrieval by name, position, issues, and topics. This database was used as a guide in designing the training program. Its more important strategic use in support of institutional development is currently limited because the project staff in Pakistan do not have the necessary familiarity with the software used for the text database.

HARDWARE

The lapsize computer used in the field work was a NEC 8201, which is operationally equivalent to the more popular Radio Shack Model 100. The daily notes were printed using one of several printers found in various offices. This was an inconvenience, but preferable to carrying a printer. As the amount of text material exceeded the internal storage of the NEC it was saved to cassette tape.

Upon return to the United States, the text files were transferred to an IBM-PC compatible computer, and entered into the text database format.

SOFTWARE

The NEC lapsize has its own text editor program, which though limited in capability, was adequate for the field notes and short reports done in Pakistan.

The "text database" program used on the IBM-PC compatible is now marketed as two companion programs, Executive Writer and Executive Filer. They are simple to use and give database management capability to personal computers dealing with text material.

LESSONS FROM PAKISTAN NEEDS ASSESSMENT PROJECT

1) A simple printed copy of all the interview notes was available immediately upon completion of the needs assessment. This is quite unusual when working and traveling in Third World countries. The more typical administrative and logistical delays in producing written material often reduce the timeliness and effectiveness of follow-up actions.

2) The interview notes were left for the perusal of several key project staff members, who were not available to meet with the consultants before they left Pakistan. (One difficulty in development work is building continuity of information when travel and communications costs are often prohibitive.)

3) The daily interchange of notes between the two consultants proved very useful as a continual point of review for the direction and next steps in the needs assessment. This could not be done with handwritten notes.

4) The resulting training design made specific use of some of the interview data within the design itself. These data were more credible because of the methodical collecting and reporting process.

5) The establishment of a text database of needs assessment material was more interesting in concept than application. The project staff were not fully able to grasp the concept, nor was the overall project designed with this intent.

CONCLUSIONS

Several conclusions and recommendations arise from reviewing the case
studies. We will discuss them and then talk more about the organizational and management experience gained from the introduction of
microcomputers into organizations. Here we will discuss microcomputers
not only as tools, but as the impetus for introducing needed
organizational changes for improved effectiveness.

1. **Introducing microcomputers into any organization requires planning, monitoring, and human resource development considerations like
any other major organizational development effort.** The validity of the
Sustainability Model presented in the first chapter rings truer than
ever before. The need to address immediate power and environmental
elements remains paramount during the early phase of microcomputer
introduction. The organizational factors surrounding the use of
microcomputers must be addressed early and continually in any changing
setting where there is technology transfer taking place. Each project
will go through the first stage of ensuring operation for limited
tasks. In general, the microcomputer is ready to become a permanent
continuing resource for meeting organizational needs.

A major level of microcomputer use in development applications is in
the "institutional phase" where one must recognize the needs to deal
with organizational considerations. Once the first system has been
introduced, whether it encompasses one microcomputer or several, it is
best to avoid "ad hoc-ing" and realize that the microcomputer
represents a major short- and long-term investment in capital
resources, time, and human resource involvement.

Often, the microcomputer is first seen as a machine to be used by an
individual for one particular purpose; only later is it seen as the
impetus for major changes. Its presence guides the very allocation of
resources. Once this is recognized, the organization can apply the
thinking and planning necessary to consider the rational introduction
of microcomputers.

2. **The use of the microcomputer for personal development and growth is
a by-product of the introduction of the microcomputer.** People of all
levels of education and background can use microcomputers. Microcomputers provide the incentive for improved performance within an
organization by giving the individual with special interest an
opportunity to demonstrate new skill levels.

The microcomputer presents an opportunity for addressing personnel
issues in terms of motivation and incentives. For example, an econ-
omist can develop a simple model for analyzing alternative cost-benefit
scenarios for a development strategy and present them for consideration, get feedback, and revise accordingly for use in making decisions
or producing a final design. The increased ability to do this rapidly
and with several iterations based on feedback can result in a new level
of quality previously unattainable. Motivation is increased:

employees can demonstrate their capability to contribute to the
organization. In addition, the microcomputer presents its own
incentive: it allows users to expand and sharpen their skills through
application in areas heretofore not applied, and build their repertoire
for the future.

3. **The use of the microcomputer disrupts current roles, responsibilities, and existing power structures--both formal and informal.**
This issue, known as "disintermediation," is being felt in an increasing number of organizations. Known as "skin pain" in parts of
Africa, the microcomputer has become the instrument of change for this
decade. Most organizations have procedures for doing routine tasks,
including the production and review process. The introduction of the
microcomputer makes it possible to by-pass several steps; the "old"
method becomes redundant or superfluous. Thus, typing a document using
a word processor and spelling checker can make a secretary feel less
important or of less value. Although the actual production of the
desired document has been improved and may be more effective, the
change in role often causes anxiety and frustration among the staff.
The use of the microcomputer to disintermediate into an established
process or procedure can be painful to individuals within the
organization.

The introduction of change into any organizational setting has always
met with resistance and if the microcomputer is a major change,
resistance must follow. If not, why not?

4. **The microcomputer legitimizes information as a resource, especially
for managers, and elevates the value of information as a resource
within the organization.** The information economy is here. The modern
manager needs and uses information to make decisions. Without access
to necessary information, the manager has to depend on gut feelings,
intuition, and personal networks of people to provide the needed
feedback. In almost every case where microcomputers have been used to
convert simple or small levels of data into manager information on a
quick turn-around basis, the managers relish the opportunity to use the
information to make better decisions. Managers want to make decisions
based on the facts; if they have no facts, they make the best decision
they can. When managers have access to the facts, they make even
better decisions.

The microcomputer has filled a gap in the management information
process. Between manual systems for gathering and analyzing data for
informational purposes and the use of large computers and "total"
system redevelopment, the most common applications--those at the middle
levels--have not been addressed. As the microcomputer is recognized
as an aid to organizational effectiveness, it provides an opportunity
to utilize the resource that has been severely missing: information.

A side effect is that the quality of data is improved. GIGO (garbage in, garbage out) often dominates whenever data is processed. But the microcomputer provides the manager the chance to address this need for pertinent information and improve the quality of data being collected.

Improved quality of information will lead to improved organizational efficiency and address corruption. This will lead to additional resistance. Luckily, the presence of corruption in a system is actually a symptom of a system that needs direction. Systems theory works here as elsewhere; a system/group that knows where it is going has more motivation to get there in the best way possible.

Thus, microcomputers contribute to staff productivity, clear understanding of roles within organizations, and adaptation to their organizational environment.

RECOMMENDATIONS

The introduction of microcomputers into any organization can be done on an ad hoc basis or systematically. If done individually, the trade-offs include organizational resistance and a general sense of "what about me?," explicitly or implicitly expressed by management, professional, and clerical staff alike. The introduction of microcomputers into any organizational setting is a change of sufficient magnitude for you to consider it highest priority. It should be given the equivalent level of resources and interest as, for example, creation of a new division or a new accounting system or combining or breaking up an organization. The use of the microcomputer is the first paradigm shift that will probably be identified as occurring across and among organizations around the world.

In a way, the introduction of the microcomputer is equivalent to introducing another management approach or accepting the need to put human resource development and staff development concepts into practice. The difference is that the microcomputer is not seen as just a machine or tool--which it is--but it represents a new way of doing things and is therefore competing with people and deeply ingrained organizational patterns. The microcomputer is totally objective; it does what it does because someone recognized a need and used the microcomputer to address that need.

The introduction of microcomputers is a long-term capital investment that will have immediate short-term impacts on personnel vis-a-vis jobs, roles, responsibilities, and relationships. The microcomputer is the tip of the iceberg of organizational reassessment: why do we do what we do, who does it, complacency and attitudes of security and opportunity. Because it is relatively small and inoffensive, the microcomputer can be used as a means to introduce better or improved management practices within the organization. The microcomputer is literally the embodiment of management into a tangible entity.

CHAPTER VI
Summary and Conclusions

Available evidence indicates that microcomputer technology is being quickly absorbed throughout the international development sector (North and Berge: 1983; United Nations University: 1984). Public sector development institutions and numerous program/project units are now using microcomputers to assist with a wide range of activities. Microcomputer uses range from those purely technical in scope, such as analyzing soil samples and processing survey data, to management and administrative applications such as budgeting, scheduling, report preparation, and telecommunications.

This inundation of microcomputer technology raises a serious concern for the international administration and management profession, namely: will the proliferation of microcomputer technology facilitate productive, humanistic, and equitable development administration and management processes, or will it exacerbate inefficiencies, unjust practices, and inequality? In this context, two issues deserve attention:

o What does current international development management experience indicate are the major promises and threats of microcomputer technology?

o What steps can be taken to increase the chances of the promises being fulfilled while the threats and associated negative consequences are minimized.

THE PROMISE OF MICROCOMPUTERS IN DEVELOPMENT MANAGEMENT

In his opening statement to the U.S. House of Representatives Subcommittee on Science, Research, and Technology in July 1982, Curtis Farrar of USAID discussed the promising role of microcomputers in development. He noted that the most important contribution that microcomputers will make to development will be the increased accessibility they provide to computational and analytical power. Microcomputers are relatively cheap. They do not require sophisticated programming training. Their computational power and versatility is increasing every year. Where the data and analytical skills exist and where there is a demand for improved analysis, microcomputers provide the potential for substantially improved analytical and planning capacity in development institutions. More importantly, the microcomputer permits substantial decentralization of this computing power to the field (Farrar: 1982).

Mr. Farrar cited several additional contributions that microcomputers may make to development: increased access to information, more timely

manipulation of information, improved planning and problem-solving, and
the ease of transfer due to the microcomputer's ease of use and modular
character. "The microcomputer can be thought of as a disaggregated
general purpose system, and can provide the developing countries the
flexibility of applying computer power to a wide range of development
problems not possible with a large mainframe computer" (Farrar: 1982).

In marked contrast to larger computers, microcomputers have several
attractive attributes for development applications. These include:

o   user-friendliness;

o   greater reliability and modular construction
        facili-tating repair and maintenance;

o   substantial versatility and power in their ap-
        plications, including the ability to network with
        other microcomputers and existing larger systems;

o   portability (with little or no additional cost or
        trouble), both domestically and internationally;
        and

o   relative inexpensive price, ranging from $1,000 to
        $5,000, for a complete hardware and software
        system.

Microcomputers are considerably more popular than mini and mainframe
computers. To the busy and committed development professional, the
microcomputer also has a strong personal appeal. Hardware and software
components have now been developed to the point where they can quickly
assist in carrying out technical and administrative tasks more
efficiently with improved results. While the evidence on microcomputer
costs, feasibility, and benefits in developing countries is not
exclusively supportive, there is substantial reason to believe that
microcomputers are able to assist in the performance of tasks at the
individual, unit, and organizational levels. The most obvious
improvements to date are evident in handling routine, tedious, and
time-consuming tasks associated with accounting, word processing, and
filing. In this area, microcomputers can provide an alternative to
hiring additional staff--an option that must be thoroughly considered
in many public sector development situations.

The power, speed, and accuracy of this technology now make it possible
to carry out various routine support tasks in a low-cost manner. For
example, personnel can use the microcomputer to quickly prepare memos,
complete workplans, and construct budgets. This frequently releases
technical and administrative staff to assume additional responsibilities for actually guiding, monitoring, and reporting on development
activities. Middle- and top-level executive time can be freed by using
the microcomputer for data manipulation, analyses, visual display
preparation, document revision, file searching and merging, inventory

control, personnel appraisals, and financial management. Thus, saved time can be used productively to consider new strategic management opportunities and options (Paul: 1983).

The microcomputer is also demonstrating its usefulness as a tool for strengthening development institutions through initiating, improving, and sustaining organizational performance. The case of the Kenya Ministry of Agriculture and Livestock Development demonstrates one way that microcomputers can be usefully applied to upgrade a budgeting and financial system (Pinckney, et al.: 1984). In addition, this technology can be instrumental in improving decentralization and participation (Ingle and Connerley: 1984). The use of microcomputers may allow decentralization and participatory operations to be initiated and sustained by providing local units with a low-cost means for assuring accountability and responsible decision making. Indeed, the initial empirical evidence suggests that, if correctly introduced and intelligently used, the microcomputer has the potential for improving development management performance across a wide variety of tasks and functions.

The promises of microcomputers in development management are greatly facilitated by "user-friendliness." User-friendliness of software and hardware facilitates the perceived and actual usefulness of microcomputers. The microcomputer is programmed to speak the user's language. This change adds a unique, transparent quality to the technology, and accounts for much of its personal appeal (Gotsch: 1982). The new "integrated" software now available is permitting microcomputers to be even more user-friendly.

THE LIMITATIONS OF MICROCOMPUTERS

In addition to the appeal of the microcomputers, there are some drawbacks to the technology's acquisition and use. The microcomputer is a powerful tool that, if some basic precautions are not taken, can be severely misused. From the perspective of international development management, potential threats from introducing a microcomputer can be clustered in three categories: technology costs, organizational processes, and development results.

Technology Costs

In general, the costs associated with microcomputers--especially compared to mini and mainframe computers--are extremely low. However, when viewed in the context of development programs and institutions, the costs escalate considerably over time. Complete microcomputer systems, including basic software programs, cost in the range of $3,000 to 5,000 each. In development contexts these initial purchase costs can easily double or triple if: a) redundant components are purchased for backup support; b) special equipment is included to handle electrical power fluctuations; and/or c) programs need to be custom-designed for special management applications. Costs can double again if the natural desire "to keep up with technological improvements" is operating among management professionals. As new components are added, system compatibility becomes a pressing concern. Imagine the consternation of a technician discovering that a new budgeting program must be learned because the current one "does not work quite right" on the newest microcomputer model just purchased. Compatibility and maintenance costs are frequently hidden and can be substantial over time. These costs escalate in development contexts.

Finally, there are various organizational costs including staff time for learning, attention to new policies, and various revisions in procedures and routines (Ingle, et al.: 1983). These costs are estimated to be at least double the combined costs of hardware and software.

Organizational Process

The threats in the area of organizational process can also be quite severe. First, microcomputers might give staff the false impression that "objective data" and "formal lines of communication" need to be emphasized to the exclusion or neglect of subjective and informal information. Caught in the "hype" that surrounds microcomputers as the technology of the future, managers and technicians can be distracted from the inherently human nature of successful development efforts. Furthermore, the push for doing everything--communications, reports, accounts--with the microcomputer might drive out other essential organizational tasks, such as strategic planning, person-to-person networking, and learning by doing, that do not lend themselves readily to quantification and automation.

A related problem is "blind faith" in microcomputer-generated output where adequate and valid input data has not been procured. Micro-computers do not automatically address the issues related to providing adequate management information. While microcomputers offer the promise for more decentralization and delegation of responsibility, they also bring the threat of narrow specialization and concentration of information processing power. This is extremely pronounced in Third World countries where administrative power is already highly con-centrated, and public officials are well-positioned to benefit first and most from microcomputer technology.

Development Results

In the category of development results, the potential negative effects associated with microcomputers are more diffuse and uncertain. First, while microcomputers may help an organization increase its internal productivity, there is no reason to equate this with "doing what is needed developmentally." Issues of effectiveness must be addressed, and it is uncertain whether proponents of the microcomputer revolution are adequately doing so (Servan-Schreiber and Negroponte: 1982; Shirkle and Fleuer: 1981). A second concern addresses the potential labor displacement associated with the microelectronic revolution, especially in Third World countries. Leaders of the World Microcomputer Center in

Paris estimate that microelectronic technology will cause displacement
of millions of people in developing countries before the end of the
century. Finally, and possibly most important, given current trends,
the threat exists that this new technology will further exacerbate
development inequalities both between and within nations.

ANALYZING THE ISSUES: SUMMARY OF FINDINGS

There are several benefits and burdens associated with the introduction
and management use of microcomputer technology in international
development settings. The introduction of microcomputers is ac-
celerating in public sector management settings around the world. In
addition, it is likely that the international proliferation of this
technology will continue, due to breakthroughs in user-friendliness
coupled with increasing versatility and decreasing costs.

The introduction of microcomputer technology is a mixed blessing--there
is ample evidence of substantial benefit and burden. This second issue
is more prescriptive: it seeks to determine what can be done to
increase microcomputer benefits while preventing or minimizing the
threats associated with the technology. In this regard, the first
lesson that has emerged from experience is that the benefits associated
with microcomputers are most pronounced when the technology is
appropriately introduced, intelligently used, and sustained.

Based on our assessment, the appropriateness of a microcomputer system
rests first and foremost on the actual needs a system can meet, and
secondly on the degree to which a system's use can be effectively
sustained. By "actual needs" we mean those current or potential
management tasks in the development program or institutional context
that can be accomplished through the use of a microcomputer. The
potential for system sustainability is a function of various environmental conditions, combined with evident, relevant, and cost-effective
performance.

Another lesson, therefore, is that the decision to introduce
microcomputer technology hinges upon several inseparable factors. At
least initially, the critical factor is the presence of tasks that need
doing, and that can be directly facilitated by a microcomputer. Once
one determines that a computer can actually help, then organizational
and environmental factors become paramount.

Field experience has brought out another potentially significant lesson
for the international management profession. Case studies indicate
that microcomputer technology has been instrumental in leveraging major
management system improvements (i.e., in performance budgeting) and in
providing a low-cost, readily usable tool for supporting the new
systems once introduced.

These findings suggest that microcomputer technology might be used in
conjunction with other "system redesign" applications to facilitate
initial entry and provide the required information processing capacity

upon which use and institutionalization depend. Ongoing research supported by the S&T Bureau of AID is now explaining these and other microcomputer and development management issues in more depth.

Several common themes emerge from our assessment. Microcomputer technology, and microelectronics more generally, will likely have a profound impact on public sector information processing structure and functions in the coming years. Public sector administrators and managers in all parts of the world will confront, and need to come to terms with, microcomputers and other "high tech" innovations. A second theme is that "high tech" appears to be a mixed blessing which brings with it substantial promise combined with many potentially serious threats. In this sense, taking a passive stance toward the technology is no assurance that beneficial results will occur. Rather, a proactive stance is required--one that assures the proper acquisition and introduction of the technology given contextual priorities, needs, and other conditions.

FUTURE TRENDS

Microcomputer technology encompasses both tangible phenomena and also those components of broad approaches including systems analysis and information management. What we now call a "microcomputer" will soon undergo a transition into "workstation" or develop a label describing each situation or application for which it is used. The technology on which it is based will be the driving force; the inherent principles of management and understanding necessary when using the microcomputer within the organizational setting will determine the course of the revolution/evolution.

In the future, a hybrid of today's microcomputers will be used in all government institutions. They will become as common as the telephone, or the manual typewriter in the next two to three years. They will become accepted as part of the new way of doing business: the initial resistance to using the microcomputer will be overcome as opportunities are presented and recognized. The benefits will outweigh the fears of the past.

Where we found one microcomputer two years ago, we find many more today, and they are now being used in settings where their use was previously inconceivable. In each case, the question is rarely whether the use of a microcomputer is relevant: each person, and each organization easily finds a reason to open Pandora's Box. They know what they want to do, and what they haven't been able to do in the past. Now they see a way of doing it with only a "shift" in approach: the microcomputer.

At this point, the "de facto" microcomputer of 1988 or 1989 does not exist. The actual operating system, screen, memory capacity and communications capacity are still on the "drawing board." The micro-computers used today will still be used to do a variety of tasks, but the actual hardware/software are evolving. Microcomputers will most

likely be capable of extensive verbal input, and will have a memory and
storage capacity many times those found today.

Lightweight, powerful microcomputers will become the dominant systems
used in development. These systems will be self-contained and allow
access to any and all other systems being used by organizations. For
example, the equivalent of the entire encyclopedia of organizational
data will be addressable for doing research or seeking information,
many times faster than a name can currently be found in a 2,000-name
database. There will be a greater degree of integration between your
uses and the ways information can be "manipulated" through analysis,
report production and presentation. Secondly, the entire workstyle
will change as you gain ready access to colleagues both within your
organization or anywhere in the world. The cost of information will
become a factor in the future: but the value of accessibility to
information will be greater for improved organizational performance and
decision making.

<u>Organizational Impacts</u>

In the case where one to six microcomputers are used within an
organization to support its operations, the impact can be considerable.
The act of using microcomputers or a mix with larger computers changes
the "organizational set" of how business is done. On the organizational level, the change in set occurs across and among the staff.
Organizational staff members recognize that their organization,
purpose, and objective can use information as a resource for improved
effectiveness and efficiency.

A true "high-tech" application involves more than a few microcomputers,
extensive investment and change-over to modern, sophisticated machines
and equipment. This often includes extensive capital investment,
personnel re-thinking and changes, and is a <u>long-term</u> technology
transfer problem. For example, the introduction of the use of satellite
imagery and data analysis into the Ministry of Agriculture, providing
field extension workers with hand-held crop pricing information for
determining local markets to give to local farmers is an example of a
"high-tech" project. This level of change is possible but involves a
total change in organizational, cultural, economic, and social factors.

The microcomputer is truly a two-edged sword, if not even a multi-edged
one. It provides the opportunity for an individual to improve
performance or notoriety through its presence or production. It can
provide increased decentralized policy and/or increased central
control.

TRENDS/PREDICTIONS

As the use of the technology goes to the regions and districts and into
the hands of the farmers or extension agents, it will only include the
most robust, up-to-date and easy-to-use systems. They will be similar
in cost to those being purchased now, but at the same time there will

be much more decentralization and integration with larger systems. Data processing management may contribute to the creation of a controlled environment incorporating microcomputers/workstations.

The Third World countries are becoming aware of the conflict between employment needs and the need to process and work within an increasingly complex environment. Microcomputer technology will become the force behind improved worldwide organizational operation. Employment will be generated to fill new positions that have not been defined yet. These positions will be filled by indigenous individuals based on their current skill levels and as planned within their countries. The jobs will be self-motivating and build on innate skills developed through vocational and technical training and not formal university programs.

Although the current approach to employment is to define jobs in today's terms, here we are talking about the future. In the United States, the introduction of technology has led to the creation of fifty-five out of one hundred jobs, working with technology that did not even exist ten years ago. These jobs were created to meet needs based on applying new technologies to address outstanding problems, taking advantage of methodologies never used before.

These new jobs will provide the motivation and incentive for the newly educated at all levels within the economy. The previous chapter's case studies describe the training of people from all economic levels. More jobs await newly-trained persons. The microcomputer may not equally address the need for jobs for unskilled laborers but may be the source of excess resources to provide the opportunity for addressing this group in other ways. For example, the improvements in other sectors of the economy can provide the resource savings that can be applied to retrain or create work opportunities for unskilled persons until such time as that percentage of the population is reduced.

The use of Local Area Networks will become commonplace within the next two to four years. As yet, they are not ready for the rigors of development use. Standardization of telecommunications will make data transfer by developing countries easier and more reliable and each country will begin looking for a way of "taxing" data transfer, as Thailand and other countries are doing now.

The concept of human resource development will become part of the institutional and development strategy of most countries. The microcomputer-based technology will increasingly be seen as the way to complete mundane and boring jobs in the future so that people can address the more creative and socially necessary work.

The next decade will see a broad and rapid penetration of the use of microcomputer technology in the development community. The generation of students raised using microcomputers in school and college will be pressure enough to introduce the use at an unprecedented level. However, the more subtle point is the recognition that will surround

the use of the microcomputer in the management and organizational
fields. These areas of human endeavor and enterprise will benefit the
most from the impact of the improved information economy. The
adjustment to change over the next ten years will be difficult: the
level of learning and shift in perspective needed to address the future
will be more obvious than before. The microelectronic revolution will
lead to increases in both willingness and capability to deal with the
complexity of today's world.

Thus, the microcomputer is the catalyst for opening the door to the
value of information in our complex organizational lives. Our ability
to process data into useful information and not just mass data files
and the concomitant increased capability for making decisions based on
this information will open new vistas in development management. More
time, effort, and focus will be spent on consideration of fundamental
development issues, problems, and opportunities. Much of the mundane
work, dreary number-crunching, and time-consuming activities will
increasingly be done by the microcomputer and its offspring. The focus
will shift to the creative process of work, human relations, and
negotiation using the facts made available through the information
economy.

Finally, the most interesting change will be the disappearance of the
microcomputer as an entity. The microcomputer is temporary: the
improved organizational development will remain as evidence of the
existence of the era of the microcomputer: 1980-1990. The era will be
over and a paradigm shift will have occurred. The focus will not be on
the introduction or use of the microcomputer within organizational
settings but possibly on another level: information used as a resource
to interface between organizations and improve interrelations.
Although the microcomputer will be subsumed by information stations,
information-sharing networks, and the variety of electronic devices
known today, its impact will continue to be felt through technology's
future evolution.

APPENDICES

APPENDIX A

PROVIDING 120 VOLTS FOR MICROCOMPUTER OPERATION

One difficulty of microcomputer use in developing countries is power supply. Most computers manufactured in the United States require a range of 115-125 volts alternating current (VAC) with an additional specification of 50-60 hertz. There are two main ways this power can be provided. One way is to run off the electrical line through a voltage stabilizer/transformer. The other way is to use a marine or truck battery with high amperage, a heavy duty 15 amp battery charger (30/100 amp) engine starter. While running off the electrical line is the simpler of the two methods, running off the battery offers the advantage of an uninterrupted supply of power. Whichever method you choose to supply power to your U.S.-manufactured computer, it must be rated for operation within the range of 115-125 VAC, 50-60 hz.

ELECTRICAL LINE SYSTEM

```
   LINE                    STABILIZER/                      MICRO-
ELECTRICITY = 220 VAC -->  TRANSFORMER  --> 120 VAC  -->    COMPUTER
```

==

BATTERY INVERTER SYSTEM

```
   LINE                    STABILIZER/                      BATTERY
ELECTRICITY = 220 VAC -->  TRANSFORMER  --> 120 VAC  -->    CHARGER


                                       POWER              MICRO-
--> 12 VDC --> BATTERY=12 VDC --> INVERTER --> 120 VAC --> COMPUTER
```


Notice that whenever the power goes off in the battery-inverter system, the microcomputer does not lose power as it is still receiving power from the battery. This system, with a fully charged 100 amp/hour battery, will run a microcomputer for at least eight hours without recharging. It is a good idea, however, to recharge the battery whenever possible and not let it fully discharge.

Probably the most important thing to remember about the power system, whether you are using line or battery, is that if the line frequency is too low, the stabilizer/transformer will begin to heat up. When the stabilizer/transformer is too hot to touch, turn it off. After it cools, you can begin to use it again. A fan blowing directly on the stabilizer/transformer will help keep it cool.

APPENDIX B

CARINET COMPUTER CONFERENCING NETWORK

Established by Partnership for Productivity,
Washington, D.C.

CARINET uses the New Jersey Institute of Technology's EIES computer to promote economic development in the Third World. PFP established this group to bring computer conferencing to the developing world for international management, trade, and planning to assist the Third World's business capability.

Any microcomputer can use CARINET. Computer compatibility is irrelevant because a modem attachment and telephone access standardizes the signal to the mainframe computer in New Jersey and that computer in turn communicates back to other microcomputers in the network. This is done inexpensively through the use of packet switching and satellite communications. Because data is concentrated into very small packages (packets) the satellite time used is a very small fraction of the time the end user experiences. On average, a CARINET message is 1/10 the cost of the comparable TELEX message.

It is not necessary to be a member of CARINET or to have a microcomputer to benefit from CARINET if a local institution has access. Membership as of November 1985 is as follows:

(CARINET identification numbers are in parentheses)

1. Trinidad and Tobago Development Foundation and SERVOL – Vocational Training Center, Trinidad, West Indies. Jerry Pantin (209)
2. Natural Resource and Development Foundation, St. Lucia (215)
3. Academy for Educational Development, Washington, D.C. (236)
4. League for International Food Education, LIFE (243)
5. Import-Export Corporation, Trinidad/Tobago, West Indies (250)
6. Foster Parents Plan International, Sandy Sanders (264)
7. Manuel Cuellar/National Development Foundation of Belize (271)
8. International Development Resource Center/Canada (IDRC) (291)
9. International Institute for Agriculture and Cooperation (IICA) Organisation of American States (OAS), Mexico (304)
10. The Latin American Institute for Transnational Studies, Mexico, Soledad Robina (314)
11. Business in Haiti, Caribbean Basin Initiative, Port au Prince, Haiti, Criss Juliard/USAID (316)
12. Caribbean American Enterprises, Miami, Florida, Donald F. Benjamin (318)
13. International Human Assistance Programs, Thailand, Owen Wrigley (325)
14. COLCIENCIAS, Scientific and Technical Institute, Bogota, Columbia, (343)

3

15. The Latin American Institute for Transnational Studies, Santiago, Chile, Gabriel Rodriguez (354)
16. SOLIDARIOS, Council of American Development Foundations, Dominican Republic (363)
17. Partnership for Productivity/Washington, (370)
18. U.S. National Technical Information, Service, Washington D.C., Frank Post (386)
19. National Association of Schools of Public Affairs and Administration (NASPAA), Washington, D.C. (389)
20. Inter-American Institute for Cooperation of Agriculture (IICA) Washington, D.C. (408)
21. Partnership for Productivity (PFP) Trade and Investment Center, Miami, Florida. (410)
22. Foster Parents Plan/BICOL, Manila, Philippines (418)
23. Council of the Caribbean Institutions for Development COUNCARID) and Haitian Business Development Center (HBDC). Pierre Armand (422)
24. Minihouse International, Curacao, Netherlands Antilles (473)
25. Partnership for Productivity, San Jose, Costa Rica, Eduardo Ramirez (503)
26. USAID/National Agricultural Library-Agricultural Information Exchange System (504)
27. International Catholic Migration Commission, Mitzi Schroeder (506)
28. Edward K. Zimmerman, Computer Consultant (509)
29. USAID/Indonesia, David Korten (513)
30. Jerome C. Glenn/Partnership for Productivity (PFP, 531)
31. Roger Nicholson, International Training Consultant (532)
32. INTERACTION, New York, Homer Williams (534)
33. Information Systems and Networks Alfa S.A., REDITEC Project, San Jose, Costa Rica, Gerardo Mirabelli, (535)
34. Inter-American Institute for Cooperation of Agriculture (IICA), Republic of Dominica (537)
35. Transcentury, Tom Harper (544)
36. IICA, Barbados (549)
37. Alex Brown/PFP, Burkina Faso, (552)
38. Trickle Up Project (TUP), Glen and Mildred Leet (554)
39. International Development Management Center/ University of Maryland
40. Volunteers in Technical Assistance, Gary Garriott (VITA, 568)
41. L'Association pour la Productivite, Togo (578)
42. William Hatfield, Computer Consultant (686)
43. Microcomputer Clearinghouse/Thunder & Associates (702)
44. Foster Parents Plan (Travelling account), Kim G. Glenn (883)
45. The Hunger Project, John Coonrod (1250)
46. ARCO Research Center (1282)
47. America's Development Foundation (ADF), (1324)
48. Inter-American Institute for Cooperation on Agriculture (IICA-OEA), Costa Rica (1332)
49. International Council of Voluntary Agencies, (ICVA) Geneva, Switzerland, Anthony Kozlowski (1409)
50. IICA, Costa Rica, (Headquarters account), Alvaro Sanchez (1462)
51. PFP/Cairo, Egypt, Ahmed Abou-Bakr (1646)
52. Flint Electronics (1658)
53. GTA, Panama, Samuel Bern (1790)

54. Technical Information Center, Technical University, (CIT/ITCR), Costa Rica (1791)
55. Center of Industrial Information, National University of Honduras, Alberto Marin (1792)
56. PFP Manila, Philippines, Peewee Culation (2002)
57. Appropriate Technology International (ATI), Washington, D.C. (2508)

CARINET members may place listings of agricultural produce sales or purchases on FRESHNET, a computer network that facilitates agricultural marketing, at no charge by sending the notice to account 370. In addition, CARINET members may also place their business/investment announcements in the Overseas Private Investment Corporation's (OPIC) data bank at no charge by sending the announcement to account 370.

APPENDIX C

MANUFACTURERS AND HOUSES OF HARDWARE AND SOFTWARE

Manufacturers will provide information on specific products, users' groups, software libraries, and user-oriented publications.

<u>Hardware</u>

Apple Computer, Inc.
10260 Bandley, Drive
Cupertino, CA 95014

Atari, Inc.
Personal Computer Division
1265 Borregas Ave.
PO Box 427
Sunnyvale, CA 94086

Casio, Inc.
15 Gardner Road
Fairfield, NJ 07006

Commodore Computer Systems
681 Moore Rd.
King of Prussia, PA 19406

Cromemco, Inc.
280 Bernardo Ave.
Mountain View, CA 94040

Health Kit Electronics Corp.
P.O. Box 167
St Joseph, MI 49805

Hewlett-Packard Co.
Desktop Computer Div.
3725 Canal Drive
Fort Collins, CO 80524

IBM Corporation
Information Systems Div.
P.O. Box 1328
Boca Raton, FL 33432

Vector Graphics, Inc.
31364 Via Colinas
Westlake Village, CA 91362

Kaypro Corporation
533 Stevens Ave.
Solana, CA 92075

NEC Information Systems, Inc.
5 Militia Dr.
Lexington, MA 02173

North Star Computers, Inc.
14440 Catalina Street
San Leandro, CA 94577

Ohio Scientific, Inc.
1333 S. Chillicothe Road
Aurora, OH 44202

Osborne Computer Corp.
26500 Corporate Ave.
Hayward, CA 94545

Radio Shack
300 One Tandy Center
Fort Worth, TX 76102

Sinclair Research Ltd.
50 Standford St.
Boston, MA 02114

Texas Instruments, Inc.
Personal Computer Div.
PO Box 53
Lubbock, TX 79408

6

<u>Software</u>

800-Software
3120 Telegraph Avenue
Berkeley, CA 94705

Ashton-Tate
10150 West Jefferson Blvd.
Culver City, CA 90230

Computer Exchange
P.O. Box 23068
Portland, OR 97005

Computer Mail Order
477 E. 3rd Street
Willamsport, PA 17701

Continental Software Co.
11223 S. Hindry Avenue
Los Angeles, CA 90028

Discount Software Group
6520 Selma Avenue, Suite 309
Los Angeles, CA 90028

ITM
936 Dewing Avenue, Suite E
Lafayette, CA 94549

Micro Lab
2310 Skokie Valley Rd.
Highland Park, IL 60035

MicroPro International
1229 4th Street
San Rafael, CA 94901

Microsoft
10800 N.E. 8th Street
Bellevue, WA 98004

On-Line Systems
115-A Evergreen Heights Drive
Pittsburgh, PA 15229

Peachtree Software
#3 Corporate Square, Suite 700
Atlanta, GA 30329

Programming International
505 Hamilton Ave, Suite 107
Palo Alto, CA 94301

Satellite Software
International
329 North State Street
Orem, Utah 84057

PERIODICALS ABOUT MICROCOMPUTERS

Magazines are an excellent way to become familiar with current trends and issues in the field of personal computing. Both current and back issues of the major magazines are available at most computer stores and libraries. Back issues often contain application programs for specific computers.

Some periodicals have extensive advertising (good for comparison shopping). Most have "reader service cards" which enable shoppers to request detailed information on many products for the price of one postage stamp.

Typical features of magazines are:

- o   tutorials on computer components and applications;
- o   books, hardware, and software reviews;
- o   columns written for users of particular computers;
- o   calendars of events and club news;
- o   articles detailing specific combinations of hardware and software;
- o   columns dealing with such issues as education, mathematics, business, law, inventions, hardware, software, and games; and
- o   new product announcements.

The first nine listings provide a brief description of the periodical. When two addresses are given, the first is the editorial office and the second is the subscription service.

BYTE -- THE SMALL SYSTEMS JOURNAL

Emphasis on computer systems and applications, with in-depth features on hardware and software. A good shopping guide. Useful regular features including news and speculation about personal computing, information on new products, books, programs, club activities and newsletters, upcoming seminars and classes. Close to 500 pages a month, BYTE is challenging but rewarding reading.

BYTE Publications Inc.	Subscription Dept.
70 Main St.	P.O. Box 590
Peterborough, NH 03458	Martinsville, NJ 08836
603/924-9281	800/258-5485

---

* These periodicals were drawn from two sources: Stolker, Bud. MEET THE HOME COMPUTER. Washington, D.C., November 1981; and Stilwell, Thomas C. PERIODICALS FOR MICROCOMPUTERS, AN ANNOTATED BIBLIOGRAPHY. East Lansing, MI: Michigan State University International Development Papers, Working Paper No. 5, 1983.

<u>CREATIVE COMPUTING</u>

Informative journal that captures the spirit of excitement among
microcomputer enthusiasts. Emphasis is on appliance computers, games
and education applications.

39 E. Hanover Ave.   Subscription Services
Morris Plains, NJ 07950   P.O. Box 789-M
201/540-0445   Morristown, NJ 07960

<u>DR. DOBB'S JOURNAL OF COMPUTER CALISTHENICS AND ORTHODONTIA</u>

Detailed programs, projects, and hints about specific hardware and
software combinations. Basically an information exchange forum for
advanced hobbyists. Buried in the technical morass is an occasional
gem of use to the inexperienced computer user. People's Computer Co.,
the publisher, is a non-profit organization.

Subscription Service
P.O. Box E
Menlo Park, CA 94025

<u>INFOWORLD</u>

Tabloid trade newspaper for those interested in the news behind the
news about the microcomputer revolution. Useful for novices who want
more details on industry trends, personalities, family arguments, and
new products.

530 Lytton   375 Cochituate Rd., Box 880
Palo Alto, CA 94301   Framingham, MA 01701
415/328-4602   800/343-6474

<u>INTERFACE AGE</u>

Features and columns about home and business applications. Articles
are often system-specific. Special emphasis on software for small
businesses.

P.O. Box 1234
Cerritos, CA 90701

<u>PERSONAL COMPUTING</u>

Features tutorials, and programs for home use. Interesting reading.

Hayden Publishing   Subscription Service
50 Essex St.   4 Disk Drive, Box 13916
Rochelle Park, NJ 07662   Philadelphia, PA 19101

<u>RECREATIONAL COMPUTING</u>

Practical uses for the computer at home, work, school or play. Book
reviews, programming problems and solutions, product news. Emphasis on
appliance computers and applications in education.

1263 El Camino Real
P.O. Box E
Menlo Park, 94025

Byte
Byte Subscriber
PO Box 328
Hancock, NH 03449

Apple Orchard
910-A George St.
Santa Clara, CA 95050

The Alternate Source
1806 Ada St.
Lansing, MI 48910

Appletree
Programmer's Institute
PO Box 3191
Chapel Hill, NC 27514

Apple: The Personal Computer
Magazine
Apple Computer Inc.
20525 Mariani Ave.
Cupertino, CA 95014

BUSS: Independent Newsletter
of Heath Co. Computers
716 E St., SE
Washington, DC 20003

The Business Keyboard
470 Castro St.
Suite 3286
San Francisco, CA 94114

Association of Computer Users
Newsletter
PO Box 9003
4800 Riverbend Rd.
Boulder, CO 80301

Apple Pi
PO Box 34511
Bethesda, MD 20817

Access
PO Box 12847
Research Triangle Park, NC 27709

Compute!
625 Fulton St.
Greensboro, NC 27403

Desktop Computing
80 Pine St.
Peterborough, NH 03458

Creative Computing
PO Box 5214
Boulder, CO 80321

Chromasette
PO Box 1087
Santa Barbara, CA 02138

CLOAD
PO Box 1448
Cambridge, MA 02138

Classroom Computer News
PO Box 266
Cambridge, MA 02138

The Apple Guild Newsletter
PO Box 371
Weymouth, MA 02188

Business Computing
Computronics
50 N. Pasack Rd.
Spring Valley, NY 10977

AgComp Bulletin
Dept. of Entomology
Kansas State Univ.
Manhattan, KS 66506

DAInamic
Bruno Van Rompaey
Bovenbosstraat 4
3044 Haasrode, Belgium

The Computer Knowledge
Network
55 Garden Ave
Chatham, NJ 07928

Computer Retail News
111 East Shore Rd.
Manhaset, NY 11030

Computerworld/Mexico
Oaxaca 21-2
Mexico 7, D.F.
Mexico

Chicago TRS-80 Users
Group Newsletter
Suite 2118
203 North Wabash
Chicago, IL 60601

Computronics News Magazine
50 N. Pasack Rd.
Spring Valley, NY 10977

Computer Decisions
PO Box 13802
Philadelphia, PA 19101

Call A.P.P.L.E.
Suite 300
304 Main St.
Renton, WA 98055

Computer Shopper
PO Box F 380
Titusville, FL 32780

Computing Teacher
Dept. of Computer Science
Univ. of Oregon
Eugene, OR 97403

Dr. Dobbs's Journal
1263 El Camino Real
Menlo Park, CA 94025

Computerworld/Espana & Micro
Sistemas
Barquilo 38
Madrid 4, Espana

Computerwoche & Microcomputerwelt
Friedrichstrasse 31
8000 Munchen 40,
West Germany

Color Computer News
REMarkable Software
PO Box 1192
Muskegon, MI 49443

Cococassette
T & D Software
PO Box 256-C
Holland, MI 49423

CompuKids
1709 W Broadway
Sedalia, MO 65301

CP/MUG
1651 Third Ave.
New York, NY 10028

COMPendium
Epicurious Publishing Co.
PO Box 129
Lincolndale, NY 10540

Data News & Micro Mundo
Computerworld do Brasil
Rua Alcindo Guanabara —
25/10 andar
20.031 — RJ
Brasil

Computerworld/Denmark &
Micro World
Gammel Strand 50
1202 Copenhagen K,
Denmark

Instructional Innovator
1126 16th St. NW
Washington, DC 20036

Journal of Computers in
Mathematics & Science
Teaching
PO Box 4455
Austin, TX 78765

The Electric Apple
PO Box 796
Wellington
New Zealand

Journal of Pascal and ADA
PO Box 796
Orem, UT 84057

ISO World
Box 880
375 Cochituate Rd.
Framingham, MA 01701

IBM Personal Computer Journal
CRC Publishing
10057 Commerce Ave.
Tujunga, CA 91042

FORTH Interest Group (FIG)
Box 1105
San Carlos, CA 94070

Infoworld
530 Lytton Ave.
Palo Alto, CA 94301

Farm Computer News
Successful Farming Magazine
1716 Locust
Des Moines, IA 50336

Interface Age
16704 Marquardt Ave.
Cerritos, CA 90701

Educational Computer
PO Box 535
Cupertino, CA 95015

Educational Technology
140 Sylvan Ave.
Englewood Cliffs, NJ 07632

Electronic Learning
902 Sylvan Ave.
Englewood Cliffs, NJ 07632

Microsystems
PO Box 1987
Morristown, NJ 07960

Microcomputer Index
Microcomputer Information Services
2464 El Camino Real #247
Santa Clara, CA 95051

Micro: The 6502/6809 Journal
PO Box 6502
Chelmsford, MA 01824

Microcomputing
PO Box 997
Farmingdale, NY 11737

International Home Computer
Users Association Newsletter
PO Box 371
Rancho Santa Fe, CA 92067

FOGHORN
First Osborne Group
Newsletter
PO Box 11683-A
Palo Alto, CA 94306

I.B. Magazette
1306 Petroleum Tower
Shreveport, LA 71101

InCider
PO Box 911
Farmindale, NY 11737

Micro Moonlighter Newsletter
2115 W-Bernard Ave.
Nashville, TN 37212

Nevada COBOL Users Group
Newsletter
5536 Colbert Trail
Norcross, GA 30092

Micropolis Users Group
Newsletter
604 Springwood Circle
Huntsville, AL 35803

Medical Computer Journal
42 E. High St.
East Hampton, CT 06424

MOD-II Newsletter
Computronics
50 North Pasack Rd.
Spring Valley, NY 10977

Mini-Micro System
270 St. Paul St.
Denver, CO 80206

Lifelines
1651 Third Ave.
New York, NY 10028

Magatari
Programmers Institute
PO Box 3191
Chapel Hill, NC 27514

Media & Methods Journal
1511 Walnut St.
Philadelphia, PA 19102

MUMPS User's Group Quarterly
4321 Hartwick Rd., #308
College Park, MD 20740

MMSFORTH Newsletter
Miller Microcomputer Services
61 Lake Shore Rd.
Natick, MA 01760

Nibble
PO Box 325
Lincoln, MA 01773
Madison, WI 53706

NCCI Quarterly
667 WARF Office Building
610 Madison St.

Personal Computing
PO Box 2942
Boulder, CO 80322

Popular Electronics
One Park Ave.
New York, NY 10016

Pocket Computer Newsletter
PO Box 232
Seymour, CT 06483

Microprocessors and
Microsystems
IPC Business Press Ltd.
Oakfield House
Perrymount Rd.
Haywards Heath, Sussex
RH16 3DH, England

Peelings II
PO Box 188
Las Cruces, NM 88004

New York Amateur Computer Club
PO Box 106
New York, NY 10008

PC Magazine
1528 Irving St.
San Francisco, CA 94122

The Lawyer's Microcomputer
PO Box 1046 A
Lexington, SC 29072

Personal Computer Age
PO Box 70725
Pasadena, CA 91107

Load 80
80 Pine Street
Peterborough, NH 03458

The Paper
Centerbrook Software
Pearl St.
Livingston Manor, NY 12758

Midnight Gazette
Central Illinois Pet User
Group
635 Maple
Mt. Zion, IL 62549

The Portable Companion
Osborne Computer Corp.
26538 Danti Corp.
Hayward, CA 94545

PC The Independent Guide to IBM
Personal Computers
Software Communications
1528 Irving St.
San Francisco, CA 94122

Personna Computer Association
PO Box 759
Point Pleasant, NJ 08742

Proteus Newsletter
1690 Woodside Rd., #219
Redwood City, CA 94061

Oasis Users Group
PO Box 2400
Santa Barbara, CA 93120

OSIO Newsletter
1900 Torregrossa Ct.
McLean, VA 22101

Os/Tech
PO Box 517
Clearwater, FL 33517

PC Perspectives Newsletter
Architecture Technology Corp.
PO Box 24344
Minneapolis, MN 55424

Sync
39 E. Hanover St.
Morris Plains, NJ 07960

Personal Computer Journal
W. 2317 Garland
Spokane, WA 99205

Synchro-Sette
The S & S Company
388 West Lake St.
Addison, IL 60101

Personal Systems
San Diego Computer Science
PO Box 81537
San Diego, CA 92138

Softalk
11021 Magnolia
North Hollywood, CA 91601

Small Business Computers
PO Box 789-M
Morristown, NJ 07960

Sextant
716 E Street, SE
Washington, DC 20003

Radio-Electronics
200 Park Ave. South
New York, NY 10003

Softside
6 South St.
Milford, NH 03055

Syntax
Syntax ZX80 INc.
RD 2 Box 457
Harvard, MA 01451

SATN
SATN Subscriptions
PO Box 815
Quincy, MA 02169

Superletter
PO Box 3121
Beverly Hills, CA 02169

SQ
RD 2 Box 457
Harvard, MA 90212

Softalk for the IBM Personal
Computer
Box 60
North Hollywood, CA 91603

Sourceworld
Source Telecomputing Corp.
1616 Anderson Rd.
McLean, VA 22101

Systems & Software
Hayden Publishing Co.
50 Essex St.
Rochelle Park, NJ 07662

Super Star International Newsletter
PO Box 33675
Northglenn, CO 80233

San Francisco Apple Core Newsletter
1515 Sloat Boulevard #2
San Francisco, CA 94132

Spreadsheet
InterCalc
PO Box 254
Scarsdale, NY 10583

Revolution
10981 E. 23rd St.
Tulsa, OK 74129

REMark
Health User's Group
Hilltop Rd.
St. Joseph, MO 49085

SuperNews
SORCIM Corp.
405 Aldo Ave.
Santa Clara, CA 95050

Sourceview
PO Box 578
Conrad, CA 94522

80 Micro
80 Pine St.
Peterborough, NH 03458

APPENDIX E

BIBLIOGRAPHY

An increasing number of books on microcomputers for the layman are becoming availible. Due to the continued growth of computer technology, books more than one or two years old are necessarily incomplete. This bibliography is provided to give an idea of the range of books available. We have specifically tried to reference publications relative to the needs of developing countries. We have not reviewed all the books listed. Some may have been updated by the time you read this bibliography. We suggest that you review publications available in microcomputer stores to locate the most current literature or talk with other users in similar circumstances to see what publications they have found useful.

Baird, C., Putnam, K., and Comsikey, K., eds. ENCYCLOPEDIA FOR THE TRS-80. Vol 7. Green Publishing Inc.

Barney, G.O. and Wilkins S., eds. MANAGING A NATION: A SOFTWARE SOURCEBOOK. Arlington, VA: Global Studies Center, 1986.

Bennett, J.J., Poate, D.C., and Olorunfemi, P.S. THE USE OF MICROCOMPUTERS IN FARM MANAGEMENT SURVEYS. Paper presented at International Conference on Microcomputers and Programmable Calculators for Agricultural Research in LDC's, May 18-21, 1981.

Berge, N. REPORT ON THE STATUS OF MICROCOMPUTERS IN NEPAL. Washington, D.C.: DPMC/OICD/USDA. 1982.

Berge, N., and North, C. FIELD USE OF MICROCOMPUTERS IN AID-FUNDED PROJECTS. Alexandria, VA: Thunder & Associates. 1983, Released June, 84.

Berge, N. SURVEY OF MICROCOMPUTER USE BY USAID AND USDA PERSONNEL WORKING IN DEVELOPING COUNTRIES: A PRELIMINARY ANALYSIS. Paper presented at International Conference on Microcomputers and Programmable Calculators for Agricultural Research in LDC's. Michigan State University, 1981.

Berge, N. BENEFIT-COST ANALYSIS OF USING MICOCOMPUTERS IN RURAL HOSPITALS. Paper presented at P.E.C.A. Chogoria Hospital Dissemination Workshop on the Introduction of Microcomputers. February 25-27, 1986.

Berge, N. MICROCOMPUTERS IN DEVELOPMENT--MYTHS AND REALITIES. DEVELOPMENT INTERNATIONAL, September-October, 1986.

Bertoli, F. and Bertoli, S. THE UTILITY AND POTENTIAL APPLICATIONS OF MICROCOMPUTERS IN DATA PROCESSING AND ANALYSIS: A REPORT ON OPERATIONAL SUPPORT IN RABAT, MOROCCO. Supported by the U.S. Agency for International Development (AID/DSPE-C-0053). 1981.

16

Bhalla, A., James, D. and Stevens, Y., eds. BLENDING OF NEW AND TRADITIONAL TECHNOLOGIES. Dublin, Tycooly International Publishing Limited, 1984.

Boardman, T.J. THE FUTURE OF STATISTICAL COMPUTING ON DESK TOP COMPUTERS. THE AMERICAN STATISTICIAN, Vol. 36, 49-58. February, 1982.

Brand, S., ed. WHOLE EARTH SOFTWARE CATALOG. Garden City, N.Y. Quantum Press/Doubleday. 1984.

Brodman, J. MICROCOMPUTER ADOPTION IN DEVELOPING COUNTRIES: OLD MANAGEMENT STYLES AND NEW INFORMATION SYSTEMS. A CASE STUDY OF MICROCOMPUTER ADOPTION IN KENYA AND INDONESIA. Cambridge, MA: Harvard Institute for International Development, April, 1985.

Brown, C. THE MINICOMPUTER SIMPLIFIED: AN EXECUTIVE GUIDE TO THE BASICS. The Free Press, McMillan Co.

Bruce, R. SOFTWARE DEBUGGING FOR MICROCOMPUTERS. Reston, VA: Reston Publishing Co., 1980.

Cohen, J.M. and Hook, R.M. DISTRICT DEVELOPMENT PLANNING IN KENYA. Nairobi, Kenya: Kenya Rural Planning Project, Ministry of Finance and Planning, January, 1986.

Covert, R. and Green D. THE BUDGET FOR THE GOVERNMENT OF KENYA, SYSTEMS AND COMPUTER DESIGN. Prepared for the Ministry of Finance. Alexandria, VA: Thunder & Associates, 1985.

Crawford, E.W. SENEGAL AGRICULTURAL RESEARCH AND PLANNING PROJECT. Michigan State University, May 18, 1982.

DPMC/USDA, PROPLAN/IICA and IDMC/UMCP. GUIDANCE SYSTEM IMPROVEMENT: AN EMERGING APPROACH FOR MANAGING AGRICULTURAL IMPROVEMENT AND RURAL DEVELOPMENT. Working Draft. 1983.

Daley, J. HEARINGS ON MICRO COMPUTERS FOR DEVELOPMENT. Memo to LEG, Michelle Laxalt, June 8, 1982.

Duffin, M. HOW TO GUARD AGAINST ERROR. DESKTOP COMPUTING. November, 1981.

Edoo, B. USE OF A MICRO-COMPUTER TO PROCESS AND ANALYZE AGRICULTURAL DATA IN JAMAICA. Paper presented at International Conference on Microcomputers and Programmable Calculators for Agricultural Research in LDC's. Michigan State University, May, 1982.

Emke, R. PROJECT MANAGEMENT BY COMPUTER. 1984.

Farrar, D. STATEMENT OF THE AGENCY FOR INTERNATIONAL DEVELOPMENT ON MICROCOMPUTERS AND DEVELOPING COUNTRIES. Subcommittee on Investigations and Oversight and the Subcommittee on Science, Research and Technology of the Committee on Science and Technology. July, 1982.

Flores, I. and Terry, C. MICROCOMPUTER SYSTEMS. New York: Van Nostrand Reinhold, 1982.

Gabel, D. TEACH YOUR TRAINEES BY COMPUTER. PERSONAL COMPUTING, January, 1982.

Gotleib, C.C. and Borodin, A. SOCIAL ISSUES IN COMPUTING. New York: Academic Press, 1973.

Gotsch, D. FINAL REPORT: IMPROVING THE MANAGEMENT OF FOOD SECURITY SYSTEMS. Palo Alto, CA: Gotsch Associates, Inc., 1982.

Grillo, J.P. and Robertson, J.D. MICROCOMPUTER POWER: DATA MANAGEMENT TECHNIQUES. (Microcomputer Power Ser.) Dubuque, IO: Wm. C. Brown Co., 1981.

Hamilton, S.S., et al. MICROCOMPUTER ACCOUNTING APPLICATIONS. New York: McGraw-Hill Publishing Co., 1982.

Harvard Institute for International Development, President and Fellows of Harvard College. RESOURCE MANAGEMENT FOR RURAL DEVELOPMENT. Cambridge, MA: August, 1985.

Hermann, C. QUANTITATIVE DATA FOR RURAL DEVELOPMENT: OPTIONS FOR IMPROVEMENTS IN AID. Paper prepared for AID/PPD/PDPR/RD. January, 1982.

Hurtubise, R. MANAGING INFORMATIONS: CONCEPTS AND TOOLS. Hartford, CT: Kumarian Press. 1984.

Ingle, M.D. APPROPRIATE MANAGEMENT TECHNOLOGY. Paper presented at the ASPA National Conference, Detroit. 1981.

Ingle, M.D. and Connerly, E. Application of Microcomputers to Portugal's Agricultural Management. In A. Bhalla, D. James, and Y. Stevens (eds.) BLENDING OF NEW AND TRADITIONAL TECHNOLOGIES. Dublin: Tycooly International Publishing, 1984.

Ingle, M.D., and Smith, K.A. MICROCOMPUTERS AND AGRICULTURAL ORGANIZATIONS: MANAGEMENT APPLICATIONS IN DEVELOPING COUNTRIES. (Miscellaneous Publications Series No. 486). San Jose, Costa Rica: Inter-American Institute for Cooperation on Agriculture, 1984.

Ingle, M.D., and Smith, K.A. MICROCOMPUTER TECHNOLOGY AND INTERNATIONAL DEVELOPMENT MANAGEMENT: AN ASSESSMENT OF PROMISES AND THREATS. Working Paper. International Development Management Center, University of Maryland, College Park, MD, July, 1984.

Kettering, M. SOME USES OF MICROCOMPUTERS FOR RURAL DEVELOPMENT PROJECTS: REFLECTIONS FOR THE THAILAND NERAD PROJECT. Thailand: USAID, 1982.

Kraemer, K. L. LOCAL GOVERNMENT, INFORMATION SYSTEMS, AND TECHNOLOGY TRANSFER: EVALUATING SOME COMMON ASSERTIONS ABOUT TRANSFER OF COMPUTER APPLICATIONS. Irvine, CA: University of California, 1976.

Lanpher, B.F. UTILIZATION OF STAND-ALONE COMPUTER-TYPE TECHNOLOGY IN AGRICULTURAL DECISION-MAKING AND THE EXTENSION SERVICE ROLE. Paper presented at the Symposium on Programmable Calculators and Minicomputers in Agriculture Decision-making, Hot Spring.

Management Development Working Group. MANAGEMENT DEVELOPMENT STRATEGY PAPER: AID'S RESPONSE TO THE IMPLEMENTATION NEEDS OF 1980'S. Washington, D.C.: Office of Rural Development and Development Administration, Development Support Bureau, USAID.

Mann, C. SHOULD WE THROW THE MAN AN APPLE? MICROCOMPUTERS IN TUNISIA. Paper presented at the International Conference on Microcomputers for Agricultural Research. Michigan State University: E. Lansing, MI, 1982.

Mayo-Smith, I. and Ruther, N. MANAGING INFORMATION: INTERNATIONAL CASE STUDIES. West Hartford, CT., Kumarian Press, 1984.

McGrann, J.M. and Griffin, S.C. MICROCOMPUTER PROGRAM DOCUMENTATION AND SOFTWARE EVALUATION. College Station, TX: Texas A&M University, 1981.

McGrann, J.M. APPLICATIONS OF COMPUTERS IN THE BEEF CATTLE INDUSTRY. Paper prepared for the Computer Applications to the Beef Cattle Industry Seminar, sponsored by the Cooperative Extension Services of the Great Plains. Wichita, KS, 1981.

McGrann, J.M. INTRODUCTION TO COMPUTERS: DO YOU REALLY NEED ONE ON YOUR FARM? College Station TX: Texas A&M University, 1981.

McGrann, J.M. MICROCOMPUTER USE IN FARM AND RANCH MANAGEMENT. College Station, TX: Texas A&M University, 1981.

McGrann, J.M. and Griffin, S.C. MICROCOMPUTER ENTERPRISE BUDGET GENERATOR SYSTEM. Paper presented at International Conference on Microcomputers and Programmable Calculators for Agricultural Research on LDC's. Michigan State University: E. Lansing, MI, 1982.

McWilliams, F. and Russell, L. NAILING DOWN THOSE SERVICE SOLUTIONS. PERSONAL COMPUTING, November, 1981.

Ministry of Economic Planning and Development. RURAL PLANNING PROJECT PROGRESS REPORT. Nairobi, Kenya: Kenya Rural Project, January-August, 1983.

Ministry of Finance and Planning. KENYA RURAL PLANNING PROJECT PHASE II DOCUMENTATION LIST. Nairobi, Kenya: Ministry of Finance and Planning, June, 1981-March, 1985.

Moris, J.R. MANAGING INDUCED RURAL DEVELOPMENT. Bloomington, IN: International Development Institute, 1981.

Morss, E.R. and Gow, D. INTEGRATED RURAL DEVELOPMENT: NINE CRITICAL IMPLEMENTATION PROBLEMS. Washington, DC: Development Alternatives, Inc., 1981.

Munasinghe, M., Dow, M., and Fritz, J., eds. MICROCOMPUTERS FOR DEVELOPMENT: ISSUES AND POLICY. Colombo, Sri Lanka, A CINTEC-NAS Publication, 1985.

Myers, R.E. APPLE COMPUTER. (Microbooks Technical Serv.) Reading, MA: Addison-Wesley Publishing Co, 1982.

Myers, R. MICROCOMPUTER GRAPHICS. Reading, MA: Addison-Wesley Publishing Co., 1982.

Newell, S.B. INTRODUCTION TO MICROCOMPUTING. New York: Harper and Row Publishers, 1982.

Osborne, A. and Brunell, D. INTRODUCTION TO MICROCOMPUTERS: THE BEGINNERS BOOK. New York: Osborne/McGraw-Hill Book Co., 1982.

Osborne, A. RUNNING WILD: THE NEXT INDUSTRIAL REVOLUTION. New York: Osborne/McGraw-Hill Book Co., 1979.

Papert, S. MIND-STORMS: CHILDREN, COMPUTERS, AND POWERFUL IDEAS. New York: Basic Books, 1980.

Paul, S. MANAGING DEVELOPMENT PROGRAMS, THE LESSONS OF SUCCESS. Boulder, CO: Westview Press, 1982.

Paul, S. STRATEGIC MANAGEMENT OF DEVELOPMENT PROGRAMMES. Geneva, Switzerland: International Labour Office, 1983.

Pinckney, T.C., Cohen, J.M. and Leonard, D.K. MICROCOMPUTERS AND FINANCIAL MANAGEMENT IN DEVELOPMENT MINISTRIES: EXPERIENCE FROM KENYA (Development Discussion Paper No. 169). Cambridge, MA.: Harvard Institute for International Development, 1984.

Poirot, J. and Retzlaff. MICROCOMPUTER WORKBOOK: PET COMMODORE EDITION. Austin, TX: Sterling Swift, 1981.

Rada, J.F. THE MICROELECTRONICS REVOLUTION: IMPLICATIONS FOR THE THIRD WORLD. DEVELOPMENT DIALOGUE, 1981.

Radnor, M. PROSPECTS OF MICROELECTONICS APPLICATION IN PROCESS AND PRODUCT DEVELOPMENT IN AFRICA. Evanston, IL: Northwestern University Center for the Interdisciplinary Study of Science and Technology, 1982.

Ribyat, K. LA MICROINFORMATIQUE AU NIGER: OUTIL DE MANAGEMENT. Alexandria, VA: Thunder and Associates, July, 1985.

Ribyat K. COMPUTER SUPPORT UNDER EPRP (ECONOMIC POLICY REFORM PROGRAM, GOVERNMENT OF MALI). Alexandria, VA: Thunder and Associates, July, 1985.

Rorving, M.E. MICROCOMPUTERS AND LIBRARIES: A GUIDE TO TECHNOLOGY, PRODUCTS AND APPLICATIONS. White Plains, NY: Knowledge Industries, 1981.

Rowe, G.A. MICROCOMPUTER HARDWARE, OPERATING SYSTEMS AND LANGUAGES. IS THERE AN INDUSTRY STANDARD? Presented at the Symposium on Microcomputer Application: Hardware Trends, Software Documentation, Professional Reward and States' Activities at American Agricultural Economics Association. Clemson University: July 27, 1981.

Rural Planning Department. KENYA DISTRICT MICROCOMPUTER EXPERIENCE. Nairobi, Kenya: Ministry of Finance and Planning, June–August, 1985 (first report), September–December, 1985 (second report).

Sadowsky, G. THE INTRODUCTION OF MICROCOMPUTERS IN DEVELOPING COUNTRIES BY THE UNITED NATIONS SECRETARIAT: SOME INITIAL EXPERIENCE AND OBSERVATIONS. Paper presented at International Conference on Microcomputers and Programmable Calculators for Agricultural Research in LCD's. E. Lansing, MI: Michigan State University, May 18–21, 1982.

Schware, R. and Trembour, A. BACK TO BASICS: RETHINKING MICROCOMPUTER TECHNOLOGY TRANSFER TO DEVELOPING COUNTRIES. Draft copy. 1984.

Servan-Schreiber, J.J. and Negropote, N. WORLD CENTER FOR INFORMATION AND HUMAN RESOURCES: MISSIONS AND PROGRAMS (1982–83). Paris, France: 1982.

Shay, L. MICROCOMPUTERS IN DEVELOPMENT--A CHECKLIST FOR SUCCESS. DEVELOPMENT INTERNATIONAL. November–December, 1986.

Shrkie, R., and Fleury, J. DEVELOPMENT IN MINIATURE: WILL DEVELOPING COUNTRIES USE MICROELECTRONICS--OR BE USED BY THEM? The IDRC Reports, 10. 1981.

Smith, K.A. and Tenney, C.A. CONSIDERATIONS FOR MICROCOMPUTER USE IN DEVELOPMENT MANAGEMENT: A REVIEW OF SELECTED ARTICLES. International Development Management Center, University of Maryland, College Park, MD, April, 1985.

Smucker, A.J. MICROCOMPUTER APPLICATIONS IN AGRICULTURAL TEACHING. Paper presented at International Conference on Microcomputers and Programmable Calculators for Agricultural Research in LDC's. E. Lansing, MI: Michigan State University, 1982.

Solomon, M.J. TECHNOLOGIES IN THE IMPROVEMENT OF THIRD WORLD MANAGEMENT. Paper presented at the Graduate School of Public and International Affairs at the University of Pittsburg. September, 1981.

Steele, R.J. UTILIZATION OF MICRO-COMPUTERS TO PROCESS AGRICULTURAL AND ECONOMIC SURVEY DATA IN DEVELOPING COUNTRIES: A SUMMARY OF THE ACTIVITIES OF THE STATISTICAL REPORTING SERVICE. Paper presented at International Conference on Microcomputers and Programmable Calculators for Agricultural Research in LCD's. E. Lansing, MI: Michigan State University, May 18-21, 1982.

Stephens, A.J. MICROCOMPUTERS IN DEVELOPING COUNTRIES. Adopted from personal communications with Michael T. Weber. Reading: University of Reading, 1982.

Stevens, R.D. and Kelly, V.A. COMPARISONS AND NOTES FOR APPLE, TRS-80 AND CP/M MICROCOMPUTERS. East Lansing, MI: Michigan State University Staff Paper #82-32, May, 1982.

Stilwell, T. PERIODICALS FOR MICROCOMPUTERS, AN ANNOTATED BIBLIOGRAPHY. East Lansing, MI: Michigan State University International Development Papers, Working Paper No. 5, 1983.

Stilwell, T. and Stambuk A. and Vera, R. THE AGRICULTURAL STATISTICAL ANALYSIS SYSTEM. Paper presented at International Conference on Microcomputers and Programmable Calculators for Agricultural Research in LDC's. E. Lansing, MI: May 1982, Michigan State University, May, 1982.

Strain, J.R., annd Fieser, S. UPDATED INVENTORY OF AGRICULTURAL COMPUTER PROGRAMS AVAILABLE FOR EXTENSION USE. Washington, D.C.: USDA, March, 1982.

THE GUIDE TO SOFTWARE FOR DEVELOPING COUNTRIES. IBM. 1985.

Thunder and Associates. MICROS IN MANAGEMENT: A REPORT FROM THE MICROCOMPUTER CLEARINGHOUSE, Newsletters 1-5. Alexandria, VA: Thunder and Associates, 1984-1985.

Thunder and Associates. PROCEEDINGS OF P.C.E.A. CHOGOGIA HOSPITAL DISSEMINATION WORKSHOP ON THE INTRODUCTION OF MICROCOMPUTERS. February 25-27, 1986.

Tocci, R. and Laskowski, L. MICROPROCESSORS AND MICROCOMPUTERS: HARDWARE AND SOFTWARE. Englewood Cliffs, NJ: Prentice-Hall, Inc., 1982.

Tottle, G.P. and Robson, F. COMPUTING REQUIREMENTS OF DEVELOPMENT AUTHORITIES IN THE SMALLHOLDER SECTOR. Paper presented at AAU/BCS meeting on The Use of Computers in the Planning, Implementation and Monitoring of Small Farmer Development Programmes. August 12, 1981.

U.S. House of Representatives. HEARING ON MEASURES TO ADDRESS IMPACT OF COMPUTER TECHNOLOGY ON LESSER DEVELOPED COUNTRIES. Science, Research and Technology Subcommittee, Committee on Science and Technology.

UNIPO, MICROELECTRONICS MONITOR, UNIPO (Quarterly) TECHNOLOGY PROGRAM. Vienna, Austria

United Nations, Department of Technical Cooperation for Development. STATISTICAL INFORMATION PROCESSING PLAN, KENYA. PROJECT FINDINGS AND RECOMMENDATIONS, New York, 1985.

University of Nebraska. MICROCOMPUTERS ON THE FARM: PROCEEDINGS OF A FARM MANAGEMENT EXTENSION WORKSHOP. Lincoln, NB: University of Nebraska, July, 1981.

Vaill, P.B. THE PURPOSING OF HIGH-PERFORMING SYSTEMS. ORGANIZATIONAL DYNAMICS. 1982.

Weber, J.R. USERS GUIDE TO THE IBM PERSONAL COMPUTER. (WSI's How to Use Your Microcomputer Ser.) Gates Mills, OH: Fire Arms Corp. 1982.

Wescott, C.G., with assistance from the Microcomputer Section. MICROCOMPUTERS FOR IMPROVED BUDGETING IN THE KENYA GOVERNMENT. Nairobi, Kenya: Kenya Rural Planning Division, Ministry of Finance, November, 1985.

Woods, J.L. MICROCOMPUTER PRIMER: A LAYMAN'S GUIDE FOR SELECTION AND USE OF MICROCOMPUTERS IN DEVELOPING COUNTRIES. Bangkok: UNDP Asia and Pacific Programme for Development Training and Communication Planning, 1984.

World Bank. WORLD DEVELOPMENT REPORT 1983. Washington, D.C.: IBRD, 1983.

Wyland, R. and Graham, J., eds. THE INTERNATIONAL SOFTWARE DIRECTORY, VOL 1: MICROCOMPUTERS. Fort Collins, CO: Imprint Editions, 1981.

Young, F.W., Bertoli, F. and Bertoli, S. DESIGN FOR A MICROCOMPUTER-BASED RURAL DEVELOPMENT INFORMATION SYSTEM. Social Indicators Research, 1981.

APPENDIX F

GLOSSARY*

<u>acoustic coupler</u>: A mechanical device that allows a telephone handset to be connected to a modem (see modem). The term is sometimes used to refer to the entire modem.

<u>action-training</u>: An approach characterized by an emphasis on in-country, on-the-spot training of persons and operational groups actually responsible for "live" development project and programs.

<u>address</u>: A way of identifying any location in the memory of a computer.

<u>application program</u>: Software designed for a specific purpose (such as accounts payable or receivable, payroll inventory, etc.).

<u>artificial intelligence</u>: A specialized field of research in computer science. The term refers to the ability of a computer to perform functions normally carried out by the human brain (such as reasoning and learning).

<u>ASCII</u>: The American Standard Code for Information Interchange. The most generally used format for representing and exchanging textual information among computers. Under the code, each of 96 characters (letters, numbers, and symbols) is given a unique binary number code (1s and 0s).

<u>assembly language</u>: A means of communication with a computer at a low level. Assembly language lies between high-level languages (such as BASIC and Pascal) and machine language (the 1s and 0s the computer understands at its most basic level). Programmers use assembly language to make efficient use of memory space and to create a program that runs quickly.

<u>back-up</u>: (noun) An extra copy of software, normally kept on file in case the original program is damaged or lost. Building redundancy into a work process by assuming that duplicate hardware or software pieces are available.

<u>BASIC</u>: Beginner's All-purpose Symbolic Instructions Code. The most used high-level language for small computers.

----

* Microcomputers come complete with an extensive vocabulary. This glossary includes some of the most common terms which you are likely to encounter. All terms on the list except those marked by an asterisk are quoted from "Glossary of Computing Terms" appearing in the December 1981 issue of <u>Popular Computing</u> magazine. Copyright c 1981 Byte Publications, Inc. used with permission of Byte Publications, Inc.

24

baud: A measure of speed at which data travels (normally between a computer and a peripheral or between two computers).

binary: A numbering system that uses only 1s and 0s. It is an efficient way of storing information in a computer since the hundreds of thousands of microscopic switches in the computer can only be on (1) or off (0).

bit: A binary digit (1 or 0).

boot (verb): Start-up a computer by loading a program into memory from an external storage medium such as a disk.

bootstrap: A piece of software, usually stored permanently in memory, that activates other pieces of software in order to bring the computer from "off" into readiness for use.

bps: Bits per second. A measure of data-transmission speed showing the number of bits of information that pass a given point in one second. In small computers, the most common bps used is 300.

break: An interruption of a transmission. Most small computer keyboards have a Break key that tells the computer to stop what it's doing and wait for further instructions.

bubble memory: A new method of storing information for a computer using microscopic magnetic bubbles. Although the technology was developed almost a decade ago, it is still expensive and not yet generally available for small computers.

buffer: An area in the computer's memory used to temporarily store information. When using a printer, a buffer is needed because the printer operates much more slowly than the computer.

byte: A sequence of bits that represents a single character. In most small computers, a byte is eight bits.

CAD/CAM: Computer-Aided Design/Computer-Aided Manufacturing. CAD/CAM is normally done on large computers because large amounts of memory and processing power are required.

CAI: Computer-Aided Instruction. Computers used to teach normally involve a two-way "conversation" between the student and the computer; the computer informs the student of mistakes as he makes them, and is able to respond to the student's demonstrated lack of knowledge.

channel: A path for the transmission of information between two points.

character: A single letter, number, or other symbol. In a small computer a character is normally represented by eight bits (one byte).

chip: A generic term for an integrated circuit (IC), a single package holding hundreds of thousands of microscopic electronic components. The term comes from the slices (chips) of silicon of which they are composed.

clock: In a small computer, a repeating signal (usually in the range of millions of cycles per second) that control the microprocessor "brain." Each time the clock sends a pulse, the computer performs a single task.

command: A word or a character that causes a computer to do something.

compiler: A piece of software that takes a series of commands written in a high-level language and translates them into a lower-level language more efficient for the computer to use.

computer program: A series of commands, instructions, or statements put together in a way that tells a computer to do a specific thing or series of things.

core memory: An outdated term for the main memory of a computer. Although core memory has been replaced by semiconductor memory, the term is often used to represent main memory.

CP/M: Control Program for microprocessors. One of the oldest and most popular operating systems for small computers. An operating system is a group of programs that is often compared to a traffic cop because it actually controls what the computer is doing by acting as an inter-mediary between the hardware and software. Any piece of applications software most be written for a specific operating system. CP/M was introduced in 1975 and has become one of the most popular operating systems; an estimated 250,000 small computers use it. Thousands of specialized application program have been written to be used with CP/M.

CPU: Central processing unit. The heart of a computer that controls all operations of all parts of the computer and does the actual calculations.

CRT: Cathode-ray tube. A TV-like display used with most small computers to show the information the computer has output.

cursor: A position indicator on a CRT. It's normally a flashing or non-flashing square or rectangle.

data: A general term meaning any and all information, facts numbers, letters, symbols, etc., which can be acted on or produced by a computer.

database: A collection of related data that can retrieved by a computer (such as a mailing list or list of accounts).

<u>debug</u>: To go through a program to remove mistakes.

<u>diagnostic</u>: A specialized program that checks the computer for problems and tries to isolate any problems that it finds.

<u>disk</u>: A round piece of magnetic-coated material used to store data with greater density, speed and reliability than is available on cassettes (see floppy disk).

<u>diskette</u>: See disk.

<u>display</u>: A method of representing information in visible form. The most common displays used with popular computers are CRTs and printed paper.

<u>documentation</u>: (1) The instruction manual for a piece of hardware or software. (2) The process of gathering information while writing a computer program so that others using the program are able to see what was done.

<u>downtime</u>: Any period of time when the computer is not available or not working.

<u>dump</u>: To copy all information available from one form of storage to another.

<u>edit</u>: To modify or add data to an existing document or program.

<u>emulation</u>: A process by which some computers can run programs not specifically written for them.

<u>execute</u>: To carry out an instruction or series of instructions.

<u>firmware</u>: A term referring to software that has been permanently placed in memory--usually into a ROM (read-only memory).

<u>floppies</u>: Same as floppy disk below.

<u>floppy disk</u>: A disk storage device made from a thin, circular piece of magnetic material. The usual disk sizes used with small computers are 5 1/4 in and 8 inch.

<u>flowchart</u>: A common method of graphically planning what a piece of software should do before the actual writing process begins, or for describing what it does after it is written.

<u>FORTRAN</u>: FOrmula TRANslation. A high-level computer language used primarily for mathematical computations. Although FORTRAN is available for some small computers, it is mainly used with large commercial systems.

<u>garbage</u>: Meaningless information.

graphics: Pictorial information in two dimensions.

hard copy: A printout of information produced by the computer.

hardware: The physical part of the computer (such as the CRT, CPU, memory, etc.), as opposed to software.

hexadecimal: A number system with the base of 16. It is commonly used by programmers to indicate location and contents of a computer's memory.

high-level language: A method of programming that allows a person to give instructions to a computer in a form using letters, symbols, or English-like text, rather than in the 1s and 0s code which the computer understands.

impact printer: A printer that produces hard copy by physically striking a ribbon and paper.

input: The transfer of data into the computer.

input/output: Called I/O for short, this is a general term for the equipment (such as modem or printer) connected to a computer and the two-way exchange of information that goes on between the computer and the peripheral.

instruction: A command to the computer telling it to do one specific thing.

integrated circuit: Also known as a chip, this is a group of interrelated circuits in a single package

interactive: Describes a computer system where two-way conversation goes on between the user and the computer.

interface: A piece of hardware or software used to connect two devices (computers and peripherals) that cannot be directly hooked together.

interpreter: A computer program which translates a single line of a high-level language at a time for the computer. Interpreters are more convenient but less efficient than compilers.

line printer: A type of high-speed computer printer that prints an entire line at a time (instead of a character at a time).

load: To put data and/or programs into a computer.

location: A single specific place within computer memory where a piece of data is stored. A location is usually identified by a number (known as an address).

machines language: The "native language" of a computer; those
fundamental instructions the machine is capable of recognizing and
executing. The instructions are represented by binary code (1s and
0s).

memory: Circuitry and devices that hold the binary 1s and 0s the
computer can access. Examples are main memory (integrated circuits),
floppy disks, cassette tape, etc.

microprocessor: The central processing unit of a computer (usually in a
single integrated circuit) that holds all the elements for manipulating
data and performing arithmetic calculations.

MIS: Management information system. The use of a computer for
providing information useful to managers (such as inventories, sales,
accounts payable and receivable, etc.).

modem: Short for MOdulator/-DEModulator. An electronic device that
allows computer equipment to send and receive information through
telephone lines. There are two major types: direct-connect modems and
acoustic couplers. Direct-connect modems usually plug directly into a
telephone wall jack; acoustic couplers use the telephone handset for
sending and receiving information.

network: An interconnected system of computers and/or terminals. The
components do not have to be physically close to one another and are
often connected by telephone lines.

node: A station on a network. A node can be a computer or terminal.

operating system: "Traffic cop" software that oversees the overall
operation of a computer system.

Pascal: A high-level programming language named after the seventeenth
century French mathematician Blaise Pascal.

peripherals: Equipment (usually hardware) that is external to the
computer itself. The most common peripherals used with popular
computers are disk drives, printers, and cassette-tape recorders.

power spikes: Major fluctuations in the electrical current that can
disrupt the computer's internal operation, or if severe, damage
hardware.

printer: An output device that produces hard copy.

printout: Hard copy produced by a printer.

program: (1) A set of instructions that tell a computer to do something. (2) To prepare the set of instructions.

RAM: Random-access memory. The main type of memory used in a small computer. The time required for the computer to find one piece of information in RAM is essentially the same no matter where the information is stored. Also known as read/write memory because data in RAM can be easily changed.

ROM: Read-only memory. Memory where information is permanently stored and cannot be altered. This form of memory is also random-access.

RS-232: A technical specification published by the Electronic Industries Association which specifies one way in which a computer communicates with peripherals (such as a modem or terminal).

service contract: A repair contract. Computer failure insurance.

software: Programs or segments of programs. The term was coined to contrast with hardware - the actual mechanics and circuitry of a computer.

software house: A company that writes programs or customizes programs specifically to the needs of an individual customer.

system: An organized collection of hardware and software that works together.

system software: General-purpose programs that allow programmers to write or modify applications programs. BASIC may be considered part of the system software; so is the computer's operating system.

telecommunication: Transmission of data between a computer and another computer or terminal in a different location. It can be done with phone lines, satellites, radio waves, optical fibers, or other means.

terminal: A piece of equipment with a keyboard for input and output device such as a CRT or printer. A terminal is used to communicate with the computer.

throughput: The process associated with transforming system inputs into outputs or products. Specifically refers to the speed and capacity of a computer, measured by the time it takes to produce desired results.

timesharing: A process whereby the facilities of a single (usually large) computer are shared by a number of users. Timesharing requires large amounts of memory and special software to make it appear that each user has the whole computer to himself.

turnkey system: A computer system in which all the hardware and software has been installed. Theoretically, all you have to do is turn it on.

volatile memory: Hardware which requires continuous electrical power to keep from losing information. Most RAM is volatile; ROM is not.

<u>word</u>: A group of characters or data that occupies one location in the computer's memory.

<u>word processing</u>: The entry, manipulation, editing, and storage of text using a computer.